A Reading of
the Parables of Jesus

RUTH ETCHELLS

DARTON·LONGMAN+TODD

First published in Great Britain in 1998 by
Darton, Longman and Todd Ltd
1 Spencer Court
140–142 Wandsworth High Street
London SW18 4JJ

ISBN 0–232–52189–1

A catalogue record for this book is available from the British Library.

Bible quotations (except where otherwise indicated) are taken from the
New Revised Standard Version, © 1989, Division of Christian Education
of the National Council of the Churches of Christ in the United States of
America.

Designed by Sandie Boccacci
Phototypeset in 10/12.5pt Palatino by Intype London Ltd
Printed and bound in Great Britain by
Redwood Books, Trowbridge

For my friends of the Nevilledale Terrace
Bible Study Group
in gratitude and affection;
and especially for Arthur, patient and faithful
leader.

Contents

II: Commitment and Obedience

Section Three: The Last Things

Epilogue

Author's note

THIS IS A PERSONAL reading of the parables, not attempting any survey of current parabolic scholarship on both sides of the Atlantic though gratefully drawing upon it; but simply reflecting on what I, a student of English literature, discover when I use the same simple tools of literary criticism in approaching the parables that I use habitually in reading all other literature.

As such I have found it a very challenging experience. For reflecting on these stories has brought me afresh to the living encounter with Jesus, his loving anger, his passionate pleading, his eye for the detail of human life, his yearning over obstinate, blind, self-righteous humanity, and his delight in and tender encouragement of the 'outsider's' tentative, wistful response to the possibilities of the Kingdom of Heaven. Most of all, this reading has brought me again to an awed glimpse of what happens when absolute Justice and total Mercy meet and resolve each other in the nature of God himself, and so in his dealings with us. Of such is our hope: and these parables declare it. In that sense they are a gloss on the life and death and rising again of that same Lord Jesus, Teller of the tales.

My grateful thanks to Morag Reeve, of Darton Longman and Todd, without whose patient pursuit over a number of years this book would never have come to fruition; and to Mrs Aileen Jones, whose cheerful – and Herculean – typing-up labours enabled the manuscript to be delivered, improbably, on time.

RUTH ETCHELLS
Durham
April 1997

Prelude

1 An Explanation

THE MANAGER OF A football club is often given to vivid expression. Among the more pithy recently was the comment of one manager, watching his much-fancied side putting on a doleful performance and losing disastrously, that watching them was 'like watching paint drying'. Sharp and vivid comparisons like that help us catch an experience in a way that the plain summary could not achieve. And sometimes such vivid analogies so catch the public mind that they pass into public parlance: 'I'm spitting feathers' to express thirst, 'brass neck' for impudence, 'black sheep' for the one in the family we are a bit ashamed of, 'prodigal son' for such a one when he comes home.

'Prodigal son' – a vivid analogy, taken from a parable, a story-metaphor told by Jesus. The use of 'likeness', analogy, is part of the colour of our language, what gives it texture and vitality. But it is much more than that; 'likeness' also helps us in everyday exchanges to catch better the other person's experience, or to understand something new or complex we would not understand otherwise. If that is true generally, it is particularly true when we think about its use by Jesus, most of all in his parables. But if we are to get the full richness available here, we need to delve a little more deeply into what is actually involved when 'likeness' or 'similitude' – metaphor – is being used.

God and metaphor

First of all, there are one or two religious aspects of the use of metaphor, or 'image', we ought to notice. For certain very strict Christians at different stages in the Church's history verbal imagery has been unacceptable: a view, based on a particular application of the Old Testament command that God's people should have 'no graven images', that such an interdict applied not simply to statues and pictures but to verbal 'images' as well. Set against these have always been other Christians who pointed out that God could only be known by describing him as 'like' this or that in some way. Yet others went further, and argued that to use verbal pictures or 'images' was in fact sanctioned by God, for not only was the skill of 'likening' a gift from God, *but it was God's own way of addressing us.*

For instance, when John Bunyan wanted to defend his book *The Pilgrim's Progress* against the strictures of his Puritan brethren concerning his use in it of 'likeness' through simile or metaphor, he declared in his verse preface that his method had the best validation, that of God's own use:

> But must I want solidness, because
> By metaphors I speak? Were not God's laws,
> His gospel laws, in olden times held forth
> By shadows, types and metaphors? Yet loath
> Will any sober man be to find fault
> With them, lest he be found for to assault
> The Highest Wisdom. No; he rather stoops
> And seeks to find out what by pins and loops,
> By calves and sheep, by heifers and by rams,
> By birds and herbs, and by the blood of lambs,
> God speaketh to him; and happy is he
> That finds the light and grace that in them be.[1]

Bunyan's aim in *The Pilgrim's Progress* was of course that of both teacher and evangelist. And in urging the Bible's use of 'shadows, types and metaphors' he was not simply stating the well-known fact that it is possible to help people understand something – such as a religious idea – they had not previously understood, by expounding it in terms of what is known, immediate, and – often – concrete; and that therefore it is a good tool for both the evangelist and the teacher. More profoundly than this, Bunyan was insisting on a *theological* view of the use of similitude, a view George Herbert had expressed some forty years earlier:

> *This is the skill, and doubtless the Holy Spirit intends this much,*

> *when it condescends to the naming of a plough, a hatchet, a*
> *bushel, leaven, boys piping and dancing; showing that things of*
> *ordinary use are not only to serve in the way of drudgery, but*
> *to be washed and cleansed, and serve for light even of Heavenly*
> *Truths.*[2]

Similitude . . . metaphor. A claim that they not only 'serve for light even of Heavenly Truths', the Holy Spirit communicating through them, in Bunyan's terms, 'light and grace'; but that through the Holy Spirit God is *himself* active in the metaphor, that such using of 'likeness' is an essential part of the way God addresses us. It is not only that imagery is one vehicle (among many) through which the Gospel is received. It is, rather, that the very nature of the Gospel is *in one sense* metaphorical, a glimpse through similitude into the nature and likeness of God. This is, of course, in no sense to reject the historicity of the Incarnation. Quite the reverse: it is to root God's intervention, in Jesus, in space and time, as a material and active metaphor for that which is beyond space and time, so that through this living metaphor we might understand God better.

The biblical 'it is like . . .'

We experience Christ's own language of what God is 'like' most powerfully in the parables: the kingdom of heaven is like . . . landowners with tenants, girls with oil lamps, the dividing of the flocks into sheep and goats, mustard seed, a wedding feast . . . Such language of 'likeness' is heard by us, of course, not only against the background of Jesus' own contemporary world (and ours), but also against the background of the Scriptures his own world used, the great metaphors of Isaiah and the Psalms: 'They shall mount with wings as eagles';[3] 'The people that walked in darkness have seen a great light';[4] 'The Lord is my shepherd'.[5] And against the background, too, of the later Scriptures we have ourselves inherited, the expositions by some of Christ's followers of what they have seen and understood: the great 'I' discourses of St John's gospel; the blazing imagery of the Epistle to the Hebrews: 'You are not come to . . . a blazing fire and darkness and gloom and tempest and the sound of a trumpet';[6] the beauty of 1 Peter: 'a royal priesthood, a holy nation'.[7] Giving coherence to all this imagery, this 'likening', is Christ himself, God's supreme use of dramatic metaphor to convey grace; revealing God in his very nature: 'He who has seen me has seen the Father';[8] the 'express image of his person'.[9]

So Christ as the metaphor of God opens up for us the very nature and activity of God. And if this is true of the *person* of Christ, it is also true of the *words* of Christ; and never more so than when he is, himself, using the language of 'likeness', of metaphor, often through parables, quite explicitly in order that we may understand more of the Father.

'Combination' and 'selection': tools to help us read

Therefore it is worth considering afresh what is to be understood, *what is actually happening*, when 'likeness', 'similitude', is being used, as in the parables, to explore a profound truth. Here we can usefully take to our aid some of the tools literary critics have developed over the last two or three decades. One of the most fruitful critical explorations has been in this very field of 'similitude', and in particular of metaphor and its adjunct, 'metonymy'. Some years ago I pointed out that if we apply to the parables some of the understandings of metaphor developed by such critics in their study of literature, we find in them fresh theological meaning.[10] In particular, I want to apply the way of understanding metaphor developed some years ago by David Lodge.[11]

He reminded us that a way of understanding what is actually happening when 'metaphor' is used can be found by looking at certain principles of language use. One such principle is that all formal language has a twofold character, in that its use involves two operations – 'combination' and 'selection'. To speak or write, one *selects* certain linguistic units, and *combines* them in more complex ones. But there are laws which govern this, and if we disregard them, we either get gibberish, or, sometimes, a deliberately shocking effect. An analogy with clothing will help us to understand these laws of operation better.

For instance, a policeman in the uniformed branch dressing for the day will 'select', from all the hats, jackets, trousers and shoes in his wardrobe. And he must 'combine' them appropriately. So, he will wear on his head his uniform peaked cap, on his legs his regulation trousers, on his body his regulation jacket, on his feet his regulation boots. When he comes home, and wants to be attired for leisure, he changes, and wears – for instance – a baseball cap on his head, a sweat shirt on his body, jeans on his legs and trainers on his feet. So far, he has both selected and combined his units of wear perfectly properly.

Now, if when he had dressed in the morning for work he had worn the baseball hat on his head and the trainers on his feet, he would have *selected* properly, because he would have chosen a hat for the head and trainers for the feet: so he had the particular meaning of such garments right. But he would have shown a defective sense of *combination*. For instead of combining his units of clothing in a coherence, a kind of sentence, which gave a clear message – 'here is a policeman' – he had created confusion by not knowing which type of clothing belonged with which. The 'language' of his garments was inconsistent, not coherent: half of it belonged in a quite different kind of 'sentence' – 'here is someone at leisure'.

If, on the other hand, the man when dressing had got the *combination* right, choosing as his 'units' the proper policeman's gear, but had worn them in the wrong way, then his *selective* processes would be wrong. It, for instance, he wore his policeman's jacket on his legs, and his boots on his hands, he would indicate he knew all these garments belonged together – added up to a coherence – but he would be showing he did not know what made for *similitude*: that all boots and shoes, however varied in style, always belonged to the feet; that all jackets, however different, covered the upper body; that all trousers, from all the different worlds and cultures in which they took different styles, belonged on the legs; and so on. So he was defective in powers of selection, and so he had no gift for similitude.

In the same way, all formal language, to be effective, requires of us the 'combination' of language units which belong together, coherent within a single world of discourse; a combination in coherence which David Lodge called 'metonymy'. And formal language also requires the 'selection' from the language units which have appropriately similar kernels of meaning but are widely disparate in other ways (like all the hats in the world, which in their wild disparity have this single

kernel of meaning – they are for the head). And this is the very
essence of 'metaphor'. So when we say, for instance, 'she has a
heart of gold' the kernel of meaning which makes that otherwise nonsensical statement valid is that gold is pure, rings true,
and is of great value; and these are the very qualities of this
woman's nature.

So it has been argued that 'metaphor' and 'metonymy', like
'selection' and 'combination', act as the poles of the world of
linguistic communication, the axis on which language-use
pivots. When a metaphor is being used, or similitude being
employed in some way, the writer or speaker is identifying
essential similarities, often hitherto unnoticed or surprising
ones, between what are otherwise different worlds. He is
bringing together the *disparate* in order to indicate the essential
likeness, and in this similitude something new or more profound
is discovered about the original subject. 'Metonymy', by contrast, is the result of the speaker or writer having an instinct
for *coherence*, for the way things relate to each other within a
single world: what belongs naturally with what. He is emphasising, often by paring away all extraneous matter, what exists
in observable and realistic relationship together. (Technically,
'metonymy' has been traditionally defined as the use of the
part to represent the whole: e.g. 'sceptre' for 'authority'; and
not unlike this is 'synecdoche', where the 'attribute' stands for
the thing it describes. Each of these technical devices can be
used as a way of approaching the parables.)

Using the tools

To make the most of these tools in approaching the parables
we need to remember that the perception of similitude, of the
genuinely 'like', in spite of vast disparity of context, is different
from the perception of what 'coheres', what naturally belongs
together in an orderly pattern. And if the two, selection and
combination, metaphor and metonymy, are used skilfully by
poet or teacher or storyteller or orator in expounding ideas,
then marvellously fresh vision can appear.

When Christ told the parables he opened up new ways of
seeing the grace and rule of God, suggesting through new
'combinations' and 'selections' new ways of understanding

what living under God's rule, in his 'kingdom', was 'like'.
Tracing how in the exchanges of language, even in our everyday
conversations, we use metaphor and metonymy, similitude and
coherence, selection and combination, is simply to suggest that
these tools are at hand to take us further into the profound
meaning of Christ's stories; tapping us in, so to speak, to the
Internet of grace. And in learning a little more of *how* the parables speak, we can learn a little more of *what* they say. If, in
so doing, we learn a little more about the goodness of the
Father and his rule – the point of all Christ's stories – then
struggling with the concepts will be more than worthwhile.

Notes

 1. John Bunyan, 'The Author's Apology for his Book', *The Pilgrim's Pro-
    gress* (1678).
 2. George Herbert. 'A Priest to the Temple', *The Complete English Poems*
    (first published 1652), ed. John Tobin (Penguin Classics, 1991), p. 232.
 3. Isa. 40:31.
 4. Isa. 9:2.
 5. Ps. 23:1.
 6. Heb. 12:18.
 7. 1 Pet. 2:9.
 8. John 14:9.
 9. Heb. 1:3.
10. In *A Model of Making: Literary Criticism and its Theology* (Basingstoke:
    Marshall, Morgan and Scott, 1983).
11. David Lodge, *The Models of Modern Writing* (Leeds: Arnold, 1977).

2 An Example: The Parable of 'The Good Samaritan'

On one occasion an expert in the law stood up to test Jesus. 'Teacher,' he asked, 'what must I do to inherit eternal life?' 'What is written in the Law?' he replied. 'How do you read it?' He answered: 'Love the Lord your God with all your heart and with all your soul and with all your strength and with all your mind'; and, 'Love your neighbour as yourself.' 'You have answered correctly,' Jesus replied. 'Do this and you will live.'

But he wanted to justify himself, so he asked Jesus, 'And who is my neighbour?'

In reply Jesus said: 'A man was going down from Jerusalem to Jericho, when he fell into the hands of robbers. They stripped him of his clothes, beat him and went away, leaving him half-dead. A priest happened to be going down the same road, and when he saw the man, he passed by on the other side. So, too, a Levite, when he came to the place and saw him, passed by on the other side. But a Samaritan, as he travelled, came where the man was; and when he saw him, he took pity on him. He went to him and bandaged his wounds, pouring on oil and wine. Then he put the man on his own donkey, brought him to an inn and took care of him. The next day he took out two silver coins and gave them to the innkeeper. "Look after him," he said, "and when I return, I will reimburse you for any extra expense you may have."

'Which of these three do you think was a neighbour to the man who fell into the hands of robbers?'

The expert in the law replied, 'The one who had mercy on him.'

Jesus told him, 'Go and do likewise.' (Luke 10:25–37, NIV)

A coherent – and closed – world

When we apply the sort of analysis I have outlined in Chapter 1 to some of the more familiar parables, some interesting insights emerge. Take, for instance, this parable of 'The Good Samaritan'. Its method at first sight seems wholly 'metonymic': that is, Jesus builds up in it a closely coherent world clearly recognisable both culturally and geographically as of his era. The dangerous road from Jerusalem to Jericho; the too predict- able attack of the bandits on the lonely traveller; his condition: beaten and naked and helpless, left by the side of the road. Nothing out of frame here; nor in the next two episodes of this parabolic drama. For 'priest' and 'Levite' would each be known as regular travellers of this road, and metonymically they 'stand for' the great and ruling religious institutions of the nation, as well as being individuals with moral choices to make. Hurrying and distanced from the immediacy of the exigencies of ordinary life, priest and Levite, like the injured traveller, the connecting road between Jerusalem and Jericho, and even the bandits, all belong together. They make a recognisable and identifiable whole: this is how this bit of the world *is*, at this time. Priest and Levite are not behaving out of character, not breaking the 'coherence' of this picture, because their character is to keep themselves from that which would make them unclean, and therefore unfit for God's holy service as prescribed by the Law. The befouled state of the abandoned victim would certainly have made them ritually unclean. So their religious and cultural world remains coherent, and they go past on the other side of the road.

The outsider

The Samaritan who appears in the next episode in this drama is also part of this coherent world; but *his* role within its coher- ence is marginal. He is no main actor in Jewish religious culture, he is an outsider. So here we catch the first glimpses of the *metaphoric* mode of this parable. For this outsider becomes the prime and central character – so that the parable is known by reference to him, 'The Good Samaritan'. The motivation of the priest and the Levite is not explained because it needs no

explaining: it is self-consistent with their roles, with what they
'stand for', absoluteness of ritual holiness as a condition of their
ministry of God's law and worship. But this marginal figure, a
Samaritan, needs a word of motivation: 'he took pity on him'.
Hence his actions of tending, cleaning, healing, raising, carrying
to the inn, supervising care, and paying for it. The inn is technically a very interesting detail, because it, like the Samaritan,
belongs to both the metonymic and the metaphoric modes.
It belongs with the familiar coherent world of the first part of
the story: but it did not appear there. The shelter and sustenance
for which it stood were no part of the consciousness of the
priest or the Levite; they could have been (that is part of
the point), but they were not.

The inn, however, is part of the Samaritan's consciousness.
For here we are in a world disparate from that of the priest
and the Levite. The metaphoric mode has taken over. Here the
marginalised becomes the central figure, one of succour, taking
risks to heal, to carry, to save, to bring to a secure place, and
to pay the price necessary. And – unlike the others – it is
adumbrated he will return: 'and when I come again,' – to
paraphrase his parting words to the inn-keeper – 'if you spend
any more I will repay you.'

Crossing the modes

What is revealed in the way this parable works, therefore, is
that by crossing the metonymic with the metaphoric mode
Jesus has offered us truths about grace far deeper than the
immediately obvious sense of the story. The parable was told
in response to a question about how one might inherit eternal
life, and what the Law meant in its guidance on this issue.
So we are not simply listening to a story describing 'neigh-
bourliness', the 'who-is-my-neighbour-in-this-here-and-now'
question which immediately triggered it. Rather, we are exam-
ining what might be meant by 'neighbour' in the much
profounder context of living as heir to eternal life. So the very
context of the parable is both metonymic and metaphoric.

In this way, the more obvious meaning of the story, that we
make 'neighbours' for ourselves and of ourselves by discerning
those in need and ministering to them, whatever the barriers

between us racially and religiously, takes on a profounder meaning when we realise that such human kindness is to be shaped by and springs from that 'loving the Lord God with all your heart, soul, strength and mind' which the Law identified as needful to life which is eternal.

And now we can trace the profounder theology of the parable. For against the metonymic, closed, self-coherent world of the Jewish religious establishment as it had developed its narrow version of God's Law, Jesus places the figure of one – One? – marginalised and of no account who will prove, at his own personal cost, Saviour to the robbed and wounded human being who, stripped and helpless, cannot help himself.

The likeness of God

The metaphoric mode speaks to our hearts. *This* is eternal life, we recognise instantly: succour for our helplessness by one who has both the competence and the will to undertake our rescue. Ritual, formal cleanness before the Law, even when its intention is holiness, cannot and does not rescue us. It is a thought to ponder on with grieving hearts as we review some of the obsessions of our churches' life. For we discover here that this parable, in its crossing of the metonymic and metaphoric modes, is bringing us the 'likeness', the 'similitude' of God himself as our neighbour. The disparate worlds of ordinary vulnerable human life, formal religion, and the Kingdom of God, are brought into conjunction, and the Kingdom of God is to be seen in interaction with the familiar world of human vicissitude. God the neighbour to humanity is characterised as 'the one who had mercy'. It is a character to which we are ourselves called: 'Go,' Jesus said at the end of the story, 'go and do likewise.' It is a call to more than kindness. It is a call to be Christlike.

Note
Some of this material, and that in Chapter 1, first appeared in the journal *Anvil*, Vol. 11, No. 2 (1994), under the heading, 'George Herbert and Parable: Similitude, Coherence and Grace'.

Section One

Parables of the Sovereign God

I: THE LAW OF GRACE

3 The Parables of 'The Unjust Judge' and 'Importunity at Midnight'

'THE KINGDOM OF heaven is like . . .' The phrase opens many of the stories Jesus tells. *The 'kingdom' is of course 'like' its sovereign.* His rule is a reflection of his being. And so we find that many of the parables are ways of describing the Sovereign God by the One who could uniquely do so. Moreover, often the story is told to set right a popular or entrenched misunderstanding of the kind of God he is. So, while each parable tends to focus on one particular aspect of his nature, taken together they give us a profound and radical view of the one God. We glimpsed something of how profound and radical, in our reading of the parable of 'The Good Samaritan'. In that story, too, the insistence on grace for the vulnerable as the 'Law' of God's domain – his 'house rules', so to speak – was the dominant theme.

Inevitably, reflecting on such a God involves reflecting on humanity's relationship with him. Christ's primary purpose in his teaching was to bring home to us the reality of our Sovereign God; but the obverse of this was to bring us home to him, to elicit from us the heartfelt right response of humanity to its Creator and Lord, to bring us to 'right humanness'. So many of the parables, as well as unfolding the nature of God, pinpoint wrong and right kinds of human response. Hence we shall be looking at two major complex parables shortly which have this double focus, on the kind of God he is, and on human response to him and how often it is wrongly conceived. Before we look at these, though, there are two smaller parables which are parallel to each other in being simply about the mercy of God. They are referred to here as the stories of 'The Unjust Judge', and 'Importunity at Midnight'.

'The Unjust Judge' (Luke 18:2–8)

'The unjust judge': actually, 'unjust' is perhaps not the most accurate adjective. He is not precisely described as perverting the course of justice: not, for instance, granting judgement in favour of the highest bidder. Rather, he is dilatory in enacting it. Jewish judges received no payment, so their attention to their task had to rest on a high sense of duty. Where a judge had no such sense of duty, either to his fellow men or to God, the process of justice was likely to be dilatory, 'delayed' at best. And likeliest to be delayed in the case of someone with no 'clout' to move things on, such as this traditional emblematic Jewish figure of innocent hardship and vulnerability, the widow.

This story is set by Luke in the aftermath of a question by the Pharisees to Jesus of 'when the kingdom of God was coming' (Luke 17:20), and his reply (immediately afterwards much amplified to the disciples) that its coming would not be marked by things which could be seen and pointed to. 'For, in fact,' his answer to the Pharisees concludes, 'the kingdom of God is among you' (or – since the Greek is ambiguous at this point – 'within you' or 'within your grasp'). The phrase was a traditional Jewish one, provoking much debate among religious thinkers; that 'God was among them' might mean material blessing for the faithful, or hope for the nation's future, or (less likely) an inner spiritual reality. In the Incarnation there is of course a fusing of these meanings, so that when Jesus uses the phrase it is at that moment, unrecognised by them, true in all its senses. His subsequent discussion with the disciples, set by Luke immediately prior to the story of the dilatory judge, takes in the popular expectation of the apocalyptic revelation of the Son of Man in the climax of history, the Last Judgement and the New Age. And the final question of the discussion is almost certainly to be found in the concluding comment on the parable: 'And yet, when the Son of man comes, will he find faith on the earth?'

The two worlds of the parable
And now we can begin to see how the 'combination' of local detail, and the 'selection' of points of similarity with the divine justice on which the local justice depends, intersect and

comment on each other. The 'crossover' point of 'combination' and 'selection' is in the common experience of 'justice delayed'. The dilatory judge's delay in giving the woman justice is the outcome not of any flaw in her case – there is no suggestion of that – but of his own absence of moral dynamic, in a system which imposed no sanctions upon him. Nevertheless, even in such inhibiting circumstances, *justice was delivered* and the widow got her judgement. Why? Because in the end even this dilatory judge found it pleased him better to give judgement than not, since the woman's persistence, her conviction that she had a claim on justice, had become wearying to him. So from no high motive save that of being relieved of the burden of the woman's constant complaint, he acted.

We need to recognise the humour in this story. Doctors and lawyers are stock figures for jokes, about either their incompetence or their venality. And the 'nagging woman' has been a stock comedy figure since the days of Eve. So we must not be too solemn about the reading of this parable. Jesus is taking a standard incident with potential for comedy, and by a sudden twist turning it into a comment on the faithfulness of God.

For 'delay' is a common spiritual experience also, given form and shape in this particular context by the Jewish hope for the culmination of the age, the 'setting right' of things at the Last Day; the Christian context of the early Church would understand this in terms of the 'parousia', the 'appearing' of Christ at the Second Coming. So the initial point of the parable is to direct us, through the human experience of justice delayed, towards the origin of justice, the One who ultimately dispenses the coming together of justice and mercy. For even in the fallible systems of human justice, Jesus is saying, where the judge is dilatory and the plaintiff a bore, the judge does actually for his own sake give right judgement. How much more then may you trust the holy and incorruptible Judge for right judgement, particularly if, like the woman described, you are clear about your need and persevering in offering it to God? Surely, even when divine justice seems delayed, you can trust him more than any human judge?

But of course the story goes deeper, and it is Luke's narrative setting of the parable which creates its lovely irony. For the profounder underscoring of the parable becomes clear when we recognise that God has already, as the parable is told, made his merciful and just judgement, and that judgement is 'among them': they are listening in the words of Jesus to the very pronouncement of 'the Judgement'. Have *they* (and we), therefore, the faith that the widow showed, so that divine justice can be claimed and appropriated, that justice which was not only rightly theirs and their nation's but the world's as well? 'When the Son of Man comes will he find – such – faith on earth?'

So the parable centres on the nature of the God we should trust: both merciful and just, giving judgement which, indeed, will not 'delay', for it is present among them at that very moment. By his very nature God must dispense merciful justice, just mercy; it is of the essence of his Being, and the judgement is written in the person telling them the story. Therefore he will indeed 'quickly', 'speedily', 'suddenly' – the word means all these – grant the vulnerable and poor (in spiritual as well as material terms) the profound 'setting right' that is the meeting of justice and mercy for which they crave.

'Importunity at Midnight' (Luke 11:5–8)

This little parable can be seen as parallel to the one we have just examined. For in both of them, though the gloss given is on the needs of Christ's followers, and the importance of persistence in their prayer about it, yet the heart of the story is the grace of the God who cannot but, such is his nature, respond to the honest importunity of his people.

The combination of details rapidly creates an immediately recognisable world. A Palestinian village of Jesus' time, at midnight. Doors of the one-roomed houses all bolted with the heavy bar which drops into place at night. Families withdrawn together to the sleeping platform at the back of the room. A belated traveller has arrived in the village and been given admission by a friend, but his anxious host finds he is out of bread – not uncommon by the end of the day, bread often being baked daily. 'Three loaves' was generally reckoned to be an appropriate meal for one person. Everyone in the village knows who is likely to have something over, something to spare. Application must be made to him. But, like everyone else in the village, he is in bed with the family and the house bolted and barred. So it would be understandable if he said the equivalent of 'Get lost!'

But here the structure of the parable, still within that detailed metonymic world, takes over. For Jesus puts this parable to his followers as a sustained rhetorical question which expects a particular answer. In sum: would any of *you*, asking for help in this way, expect the answer, 'Go away'? The expected answer, borne out by human social experience, is, 'No'.

But here is the 'crossover' point, through the 'selection' of similitude. For the disciples are being likened to someone seeking for help at midnight *in order themselves to meet the obligations of friendship*, in order themselves to care for the weary, hungry, travelworn who has turned to them at this ungodly hour. The question therefore becomes, 'Can you rely on a human friend to meet, however grudgingly, a need that is out of the ordinary, that is not your own but to which you have a moral commitment, which demands more from you than you have to give?' If the answer to this is usually 'yes', then how much more must this be true of the unsleeping God?

And so we are in a position to see a little more clearly how the parable works. For Luke sets it in the context of Jesus talking to his followers, at their request, about prayer, and the dynamic of prayer. He has taught them a pattern of prayer we now know as 'the Lord's Prayer'; and immediately after this parable, told therefore in relation to that prayer pattern, he urges them, '*So* [i.e. in consequence of all this] I say to you: Ask, and it will be given to you; search and you will find; knock and the door will be opened for you' (Luke 11:9).

Thus the parable relates directly to what we are to look for in our praying to God. The crossover into the metaphoric mode is reinforced by the word 'so'. This God whom we approach as intimately as a friend or member of the family always has resources to spare for us, when we find ourselves unable to meet our obligations under the divine 'Law'. But the parable goes deeper. For the resources are not simply there for us in our own exigencies, but for those who turn to us. The *petition* of the one asking for the three loaves is also an *intercession*, since he is asking, not for himself, but for his unexpected guest.

The parable therefore reinforces the double thrust of Christ's pattern prayer, that we are to take both our own need and the world's to God, and that this is right praying because he is that kind of a God. For, if even a faulty human friend can be expected to rise to the occasion, how could it be imagined that God, the God who is Father of our Lord Jesus Christ, would not meet our need? Indeed, has he not already done so?

For again, there is the irony in the structure of this story, that God has at that very point in Luke's narrative met the disciples' need in the person of Christ, who, begged by them to teach them how to pray, does so; and who is later to 'act out' a similar parable, with a huge crowd, two fishes – and five loaves.

So Jesus is emphatic in his parables about how wholly God was to be trusted to respond with mercy, when need arose. Two of his most complex parables take us much more deeply into the truth of that. So to them we must now turn.

4 The Parables of *'The Prodigal Son'* and *'The Good Employer'*

THESE TWO MAJOR, and complex, parables both give a radical view of the Sovereign God which challenges and even shocks. And shocked humanity appears in them, with an attitude which questions us, 'Which God will you choose? This God as he really is, who overturns narrow prescriptiveness, or the one you make in conformity with your own notions of just rule?' For these two parables bring us immediately face to face with the essential principle of God's sovereign rule: that in his domain 'mercy and truth are met together, righteousness and peace have kissed each other'. Human society struggles with such equity. But in the Kingdom of heaven it is the law of the land.

These two parables, one of them probably Christ's best known, present this law of the Kingdom of heaven uncompromisingly. The parable of 'The Good Employer', appearing only in Matthew's gospel (Matt. 20:1–16), can arguably be read as Matthew's equivalent of Luke's tale of 'The Prodigal Son' (Luke 15:11–32), which is why it is helpful to look at them together. For at the centre of both stories there is a tension between the notion of 'just deserts', on the one hand, and on the other the exercise of a generosity which seems to undermine our whole human system of just rewards. Moreover, in both parables this generosity does not seem to be applied even-handedly. So, many people find the parable of 'The Good Employer' 'difficult'; and even the parable of 'The Prodigal Son' leaves many readers sympathising with, even identifying with, the viewpoint of the elder brother in the story. In so far as this happens it is clear the parables have lost neither their contemporaneity nor their sharpness.

It is worth probing a little further here into popular reaction to these two stories. For there is little doubt that if a poll were taken, the parable of 'The Prodigal Son' would prove (perhaps with that of 'The Good Samaritan') top of the ratings. Yet, given the present fluidity of family structures in England, and the reordering of society in line with market forces, some have suggested that a good employer who goes beyond what the law requires of him, in a minimum wage for those who have previously been marginalised by society, might be thought to have spoken more immediately to our condition.

Yet it is not so. It is the father figure, going out in love to meet a wayward child, who speaks to our deepest sense of good. Perhaps it is because, most vitally, the parable of a prodigal son and a loving father gives primary weight to tenderness in the relationships (the elder brother's lack of it was a clue to the state of his heart); and this dimension of God's relationship with us we sense we lose at our peril.

'Tenderness', however, is not appropriate in the purely formal and public relationship between the employer and his workers. And this makes even more mysterious and challenging the quality of unwarranted generosity in the employer's dealings with the workers on short time, since it is not the understandable product of a father's affection. Moreover, he does not give the other workers more than their agreed due: so it is easy to understand why these argue that his generosity is selective, and therefore to be condemned. It is the same perception we have seen in the elder brother's angry words to the father. Does the father's loving reply remain opaque to him? As, for many, have such germane comments of Jesus as 'Those who are well have no need of a physician, but those who are sick' (Mark 2:17).

It is this tension which makes the perspective from which we view the story all-important. That is: is the parable of 'The Good Employer' a story primarily about the proper rights and rewards, under God, of human beings? Or a story about the nature of God and *therefore* his consequent dealings with human beings? It is the same question we need ask about the parable of 'The Prodigal Son'. The very fact that it is now so frequently referred to as 'The Parable of the Loving Father' indicates the shift in focus in our reading: from 'this is the marvel that as sinners you will experience whenever you turn again to God', to 'this is what the God who is your Father is like, so, this is how you will find yourself gathered in by him'. Discerning who the story is ultimately about helps give us the perspective we need.

Dramatis personae

The remarkable comparability between the two stories extends to the nature of their 'dramatis personae'. In both there are the worthy and hardworking, who have proper and formal expectations of what is publicly, even legally, regarded as the proper reward for their toil. In both there is someone who has not deserved, under such an agreed system of rewards, anything much. And in both there is a central figure who, apart from any natural emotional bonding, is in a formal legal relationship which has contractual dimensions either as parent or as employer, with all the others; who from his own wealth chooses to honour the terms of the contract with the worthy, but to go far beyond it in generosity to the unworthy. In both, this person is challenged angrily by those who seem merely to have received their 'due'. In both, the reply of the central figure to his challengers indicates a way of perceiving the situation, and its needs, wholly other than the fiercely exacting 'justice' or 'fairness' being pressed upon him. It is this sense of two quite different perceptions at work through the characters in the stories which is crucial to our reading of them. We shall probe this more deeply when we look closely at the selection and combination, metaphor and metonymy, at work in the stories.

The perspectives of Luke and Matthew

First, however, we need to note that it is the perspective from which the story is understood by the gospel-writers to have come – the incident which in their account prompted it – which helps to account for the gloss they give. In Luke's story of 'The Prodigal Son', the tale is told in the context of a jibe against Jesus by the 'Pharisees and scribes' – those representatives of 'the worthy' – that 'this man receives sinners and eats with them' (Luke 15:2). Jesus' response, as Luke describes it, is to tell a sequence of three stories, the first two fairly brief ones

('The Lost Sheep' and 'The Lost Coin'), each concluding with a statement (it is not a speculation) about the joy in heaven over even 'one sinner' who repents. This is the bridge into the story of 'The Prodigal Son and the Loving Father', which ends not with a repeat of the statement about the joy in heaven, but with the profound comment of the loving father himself, that 'to make merry and be glad' is 'fitting' because they have witnessed the recovery of one who was lost, the return to life of one who was dead. This is 'crossover language': taking us from the coherent closed 'metonymic' world of legal duties and expectations, into a different universe, where justified rejection is turned into loving and joyous acceptance. Where, in fact, the human death-like experience of having cut oneself off from all that gave one identity and value, so that it is as though one no longer officially exists, is replaced by the rebirth experience of being not only reinstated, but honoured, with the best robe and the precious ring, and the feasting attendant on the celebration of one most dear. As such, it is a metaphor of that 'domain' which is God's, in which we all are inheritors if we choose to claim our inheritance. (Note that there is no question of the elder brother not receiving his share of the inheritance. For in this kingdom, generosity to one does not mean less for the other.) So Luke's 'perspective' on the story starts from a context of 'good' characters dismissing as improper company 'bad' characters, but in contrast moves on to describe a *divine* perspective from which such dismissiveness is seen as alien to the nature of God. If God is such, then human 'rejects' cannot be written out of the story, for their continued life is of profound concern to their heavenly Father.

Matthew tells his comparable story of 'The Good Employer' in the context of Jesus' teaching about what it means to follow him, what its demands and costs, as well as rewards. The early Church directed this parable at issues of church order. Certainly the story is placed between the repeated statements that the 'first will be last, and the last first'. (At the end of the tale this is reversed: 'So the last will be first, and the first last'.) It is easy to see why the saying has been attached to the story, since a part of the action is indeed the last going first: but the connection is much deeper than that.

For the gospel context of the story begins in the previous chapter (19:16ff) with the account of the rich young man asking

Jesus, with all seriousness, what he must do 'to inherit eternal life', i.e., to win – deserve? – the ultimate rewards of heaven. Jesus' reply to him is that he must first dispossess himself of all the wealth that gives him position and social respect currently, giving it instead to those who are in need. It is an action mirroring the action of the God of these stories. In such a state of vulnerability, he must then follow Jesus. (Those small-businessmen, James and John, did precisely this, leaving at Jesus' call their father Zebedee with 'the hired men' to run their fishing business.) The rich young man goes away sadly, for 'he had many possessions'. Christ's comment is of how 'hard' it is for the rich (and therefore 'secure') 'to enter the kingdom of heaven'. The disciples' astonishment at this arises from the same attitude as that of the elder brother and the full-time workers in the two stories. The assumption runs: if they who are clearly 'the worthy', blessed by God with this world's success and therefore clearly enjoying his favour – if they find it hard to win heaven, 'deserving' as they are, what hope for this world's 'failures'? 'Who then can be saved?' No one, by rights, is the implication. Now they are getting closer to the truth Jesus wants them to see: quite right, no one by human desert can win heaven. But God is a God of grace ... 'For mortals it is impossible, but for God all things are possible.'

But just as they seem to have begun to grasp this Peter starts to wobble. It suddenly strikes him that he and his fellow disciples have done just what Jesus had required of the rich young inquirer. They have 'left everything, and followed'. So have they not deserved the rewards of heaven? Indeed, Jesus replies, 'at the renewal of all things' their state will be kingly, their task that of royal judges. But this is followed by a warning: it is as inappropriate to make precisely the same assumptions about one's 'just rewards' for 'worthiness' in following Christ, as for 'worthiness' in the world's terms. The point is, Jesus suggests, any versions of 'worthiness' are inappropriate: operating, so to speak, in the wrong dimension. It is the grace of God which determines the rewards. So that even among his faithful followers, 'many who are first will be last, and the last will be first'.

And then he tells the story of 'The Good Employer' to make the point clear. So in the gospel context, the story can be understood as challenging all systems of 'just deserts' as a guide to our heavenly destiny: whether as a reward for 'good work', strict and zealous keeping of the Law, as demanded by the Pharisees; as the natural continuation of worldly success and eminence; or whether as the 'deserved' and therefore inarguable expectation of those who have become eminent in the body of the faithful which is the early – and continuing – Church. To all these categories, and any other which may arise to entice us to look for 'just reward', Jesus responds by putting the emphasis back on the nature of the God who is sovereign, the only arbiter, whose judgements are especially generous to those who do not see themselves as deserving.

So the key to Matthew's perspective in his account of Jesus' story of 'The Good Employer' lies in 20:14 and 15: 'I choose to give this last the same as I give to you. Am I not allowed to do what I choose with what belongs to me? Or are you envious because I am generous?' The focus is on God's right to give as he chooses – he is Lord – and on the evil in the human heart exposed by it. There is a parallel here with the terrible story of the first murder, triggered by Cain's envy of the warmth of God's relationship with Abel:

> The Lord said to Cain, 'Why are you angry, and why has your countenance fallen? If you do well, will you not be accepted? And if you do not do well, sin is lurking at the door; its desire is for you, but you must master it.' (Gen. 4:6)

Hence it is the absolute Lordship, Sovereignty, of God, expressed in his generous dealings with those regarded by their fellows as the undeserving, which provides the perspective from which Matthew tells the story. With a counterpoint in our perception of the protesting workers as envious, which parallels precisely our perception of the elder brother – in the parable of 'The Prodigal Son' – as also envious.

And so what emerges from the perspective given to the stories by the two gospel writers is the sharp contrast in values and priorities between the 'worthy' in the two stories – the elder brother in the one, and the workers who had toiled all day in the other – and the central figure who makes the final allocation of reward. We need now to look at what this tells us of God, what we find when we explore more fully how each story is told.

'The Prodigal Son, the Loving Father and the Elder Brother' (Luke 15:11–32)

Key details combine in this story to build a coherent, realistic picture of a recognisable society. There is a well-defined family grouping: father, older son, younger son. ('Mother' would be 'contained' within the reference to 'father', hence no mention of her.) We are presented with a culture of wealth where the laws of property and inheritance are clearly defined and understood. According to the law the property would be divided as an inheritance between the two sons, and it was in order for a son to request a pay-off on his patrimony early. The estate is clearly rich, supporting different ranks of servants: 'hired hands' (v. 17), and 'slaves' (v. 22); and the excellent relationship of the owner to them is clearly sketched in. Indeed, it is the generous way his father treats his hired servants which, remembered, helps to bring the wandering son back: 'How many of my father's hired hands have bread enough and to spare...!' Moreover, the older brother's inquiry of 'one of the lads' (v. 26 – another quite affectionate term for 'servant') about what is happening, elicits a reply which is remarkably succinct, suggesting the boy has wholly entered into the heart of the occasion: 'Your brother has come ... and your father has killed the fattened calf because he has him back safe and sound' (NIV).

So the details suggest a large and wealthy estate (goats and cattle, the measure of wealth, are referred to) which has survived the pay-out to the younger son, where there are degrees of servants who are well treated. And this range of servants is important, because in the older brother's outburst he refers to himself, with the exaggeration of anger, as working for his father like one in the lowest degree of servitude, 'like a slave', disregarding the truth, of which his father gently reminds him, that it is his own patrimony he is supervising. ('Child ... everything I have is yours.') The penitent younger brother by contrast, has come close enough to selling himself into slavery to be realistic: he knows what real slavery is. So he determines to ask to be treated like one of the 'hired hands', because 'I am no longer worthy to be called your son'. So in the structure of the story there is a deliberate ironic parallel between the two brothers' statements about sonship and servitude, in which they emerge precisely opposite each other in their claims.

This wealthy property is 'placed'; there is a road leading to it which figures in the story, since those approaching can be seen 'far off' (v. 20). There are fields extending beyond it, so extensive that the elder brother working in them has no sight of what is happening back at home.

And there is the 'distant country' to which the younger brother goes. He 'scattered his wealth prodigally', to give a literal translation of v. 13. His older brother glosses this as having devoured their father's living with harlots. The hint here is of the country boy going to the wicked city, an easy target, given his self-indulgence, for the rapacious. So we have here a supplementary realism of detail, still part of the metonymic picture but extending its boundaries: the wicked city, the profligate heir, the soaking away of all the inheritance, set over against the steady slow industrious building up of wealth in the country life of his brother on the estate.

All his money is gone, and it is precisely at this moment that the city itself suffers a crisis: there is a severe famine in the land. It is this famine which creates one of the 'crossover' points into the metaphoric mode of the story. For, while it is a touch of realism, it also introduces a much profounder dimension, the theme of life and death which the father is later to comment on with even deeper meaning. For the youth's life is at risk. Not only does he 'begin to be in want': more than that, he is starving. So truly so that if only the pods the pigs were eating could be his, he would gladly have got down with them and shared their food. It is an image, particularly in Jewish terms, of total abjectness. Associated with swine, and therefore ritually 'unclean' by virtue of his way of life; and yet of less value than the pigs themselves, for he longs for, and cannot have, their food. And in such case 'no one gave to him'. It is a sort of death, total social death with physical death imminent. The metaphor of 'being as one dead to other people' runs with the reality of being near starving to death.

It is the contrast between this lack of care or help from any in his present land, and the generosity of his father's house to all belonging to it, which leads to his new perception of truth. When the issue is literally that of life or death he recognises the true grace and compassion of his home. And becomes clear, at that point, like the Psalmist, that it is better to be a door-keeper – hired servant – in the house of such a one as the father, Father, than to dwell in the tents of wickedness. The truth of this perception is confirmed when his father is 'moved with compassion' and comes 'running' to him. This is another disjunction in the tightly knit, coherent metonymic picture initially built up. No patriarchal figure would normally demean himself by such undignified haste, nor by 'falling on his neck' (hugging him?) and 'fervently kissing him'.

Ironically, as the metaphoric mode that takes us into the life/death issues of this story shows, the older brother has not recognised this truth about his father's house at all. For he accuses the father of *lack* of generosity, lack of care or appreciation, towards him. 'You never gave me so much as a kid, to make merry with my friends . . .'

The elder son, therefore, shows no awareness of the life/death issue, or the true nature of the father. The father, by contrast, uses the life/death language suggested by the famine, but opens it up to a whole new dimension in which 'life' and 'death' have a moral and spiritual as well as a physical meaning. 'This my son was dead and came to life again, he was lost and is found.' He uses it first to the servants and then to the elder brother, so that in the telling of the parable it acts as a 'chorus', underlining the meaning.

And the metaphor is built up further. For this returning wanderer is by implication penniless, barefoot, ragged. More appropriate in appearance to a 'slave' than even a hired hand, certainly not to a son of the house. So the father's calling for the 'best robe', the 'ring', the 'sandals', is not only a proper detail in the realistic coherent world of his culture: in the metaphoric pattern of the parable it is a powerful image of the father 'covering' the son's unworthiness for his role. As such, he is not only making a public declaration about his son's acceptability and status: he is actualising that acceptance back into sonship by clothing him into the role.

The other detail where metaphor and metonymy cross is that of the banquet. Like the clothing, it is a celebration of new life, of joy and honour and thanksgiving; with resonances of the End-Time and the feast of heaven. Hence the refusal of the older son, in his anger, to attend, is of the greatest significance, because he is excluding himself from the dimension of new life which the father has accorded the returned prodigal, and in which the whole household is invested. That is, it is a *corporate* act of joy. And further, the contrast is deliberate between the 'famine' of the far country, and the munificence of this household. Yet the older brother is choosing a sort of 'famine' . . .

So the parallels are developed ironically, and indeed shockingly for 'righteous' listeners. The 'bad' brother, starving in his self-imposed exile, watching with envy the pigs eating, 'coming to himself', recognising the truth of his home and father and returning to the feasting that awaits his penitence; and the 'good' brother, living soberly but comfortably, then in bitterness watching from outside in self-imposed exile and hunger the feasting of the banquet, because his self-righteousness will not allow him any sense of celebration.

The father's tenderness to *him* is notable also. His action in 'coming out' from the banquet, and 'beseeching him' is the parallel in the story with his 'running out' to and hugging the younger brother. Each son in turn has excluded himself. To both, the father goes out in tenderness. To both he indicates the profound nature of what is at stake: nothing less than new life in the face of death itself.

What then did Jesus tell us, through the structure of this parable, about the God who is his Father? That he is a tender God, who like the father of the story comes out to meet us when we are 'far off' and in the most beggarly of conditions (including spiritual condition). And that this God also comes out to meet us when in the anger of wounded self-esteem, even self-righteousness, we exclude ourselves from the life of God's domain which the 'banquet' suggests, where the compassion and love of God sits others down at table with us whom we would ourselves exclude.

There is therefore no rejection at all here of the worth of the older son. But there is a very strong warning, that God's sovereign rule of grace is not determined by 'just deserts', but by divine tenderness and compassion. And that this is the very nature of 'heaven', and the disapproval of the (self)righteous may not change it. The tender father yearns over the self-righteous older brother *as much as* over the wandering younger one. The tragic dimension, spiritually, of the story is that the older brother does not recognise he is giving just cause for yearning. The story challenged directly the religious authorities of Christ's day but it continues to bite wherever, as Emily Bronte once put it, we search the Bible (and the God it declares) for promises to ourselves and curses to our neighbours.

If, therefore, as elder brothers we are not at God's banquet finally, it will be by self-exclusion from a celebration which the self-righteous heart cannot comprehend or accept. And – final irony – we do not know the end of this story. We do not know whether the older brother will hear his father, and come in. We know what many of the 'older brothers' of Christ's own day did. They condemned him, and with him all prodigal sons. And by so doing stood outside the banquet.

But we who are 'older brothers' in our own day: will we come in? For the story is still incomplete . . .

'The Good Employer' (Matt. 20:1–16)

In the setting of this parable we find, as usual in Christ's stories, first of all a closely observed, coherent, metonymic world, self-consistent in its nature. There are two familiar locations in the story, which belong to the same world: one, the public marketplace, where most of the discussion takes place; and the other, the vineyard, so to speak 'off-stage', which is the focus of the negotiations. There are certain details which would be known by implication to Jesus' audience which he would not need, therefore, to state. For instance, that harvest time of grain or grape was the only time of the year when unskilled labourers would thus be gathered for hire in the marketplace, because only then were extra hands needed. So the implicit context of this story is the time of harvesting.

This hidden detail has some significance in the language of metaphor of the story, as we shall see. Then again, the terms of work and wages were 'usual' – a denarius for a full day's work – to be paid always at the end of the day unless the employer was committed to employing the worker for further work the next day. This was 'usual' because prescribed in Leviticus (19:13) where there is a humane insistence on casual labourers getting their money by nightfall, for the obvious reason, presumably, that they would then be sure to be able to afford a meal and a bed: 'The wages of a hired servant shall not remain with you all night until the morning.'

So a coherent world of an ordered agrarian society begins to emerge here. The local contexts in which we define our human lives, those of time and space, are clearly identified. It is the world of Jesus' contemporary hearers, at the time of the harvesting of the grapes, on one particular day in one particular town with its marketplace, vineyards, wealthy owners, managers and casual labour force. And the hours of the working day grind past slowly, giving the movement to the whole story: six a.m.; nine a.m.; twelve noon; three p.m.; five p.m. (the 'eleventh hour'); and six p.m., the end of the working day. Then it is pay time, and the men are summoned by the manager to receive their wages: lined up in an orderly way. Presumably the owner is present, looking on, since he is available to respond to the grumbling. A clear, detailed picture, therefore, of our little local human world at a particular moment. The economic and social routines well established so as to be 'fair'.

But cutting across this coherent and completely recognisable picture – recognisable socially even twenty centuries of human history later – is another kind of language. The first hint of it, I suppose, is present in the owner's conversation with the men still waiting in the marketplace at five o'clock in the evening. The reason for their idleness, he elicits, is not unwillingness but lack of opportunity: 'Because no one has hired us'. Common sense on their part would have told them no one would hire them so late in the day, so they might as well go home. But they didn't. Instead, they were going to see out the full working day, simply waiting. This particular group, sketched in so skilfully in a few strokes by Jesus, have also 'borne the burden of the day, and the scorching heat' – to quote the grumblers later – but with a very different burden: the sick sense of not being chosen, of having nothing to show for the hours looking for work. 'The stature of waiting.' It is a condition of life we have begun to reflect on in our own times as having profound things to say to us spiritually.

When the owner sends them, even so late, to his vineyard, his action again cuts across the orderly pattern of this carefully balanced society. Can extra hands be useful at this point? Possibly. It is harvest-time: the work must be completed. That is one possible line of interpretation. And – if the owner's concern is as much for the men as for the work – if they do not work now, harvest will be complete and they will have lost the final opportunity to share in its abundance. The interesting aspect of both these lines of thought is that implicit in them is the notion of 'End-Time': and this begins to direct us to the fuller theological meaning of the story. (Particularly when we remember that the 'vine' often represented the chosen people of God.) But the clearest disjunction to the pattern of this ordered world comes when the employer tells the manager to pay the last-comers first. This is so blatant an overturning of the accepted order of things that it is clear some different system of values is being introduced. And so the generous pay – that appropriate to a full day's work – fits with this. And with it, raised expectation from those who have toiled throughout the day. Yet when they get their pay it seems in no way to answer to a different set of values. They get what they agreed, and no more. The language of their protest, however, is significant. It is not that of the formal institutionalised agreements of their society, or even more abstractly 'the Law'. Instead, it engages, but negatively so, with precisely the same issues of being personally valued that lie behind the actions of the generous employer to the disheartened men of the 5 o'clock marketplace. Which lay also behind the action of the loving father towards his prodigal son in Luke's parable. For, just like the elder brother in that story, the complaining workers are bitter because someone they think undeserving has been 'valued' equally with them: 'These last have worked only one hour, and you have made them equal to us who have borne the burden of the day, and the scorching heat.' It is not only money but *principle* they see as at stake. So, indeed there is a principle at work. The same principle, precisely, which made the elder brother recount his hard and faithful labour for his father as a reason for anger at his father's generosity to someone who also had not 'borne the burden of the day, and the scorching heat'.

So the two worlds, of formal contracts, and of personal worth, are now exposed by these two different kinds of language: that of the small metonymic world where there is tight control, legal agreement, and 'measurability': and that of the metaphoric world where the very basis of that legal agreement is forcibly revisited. The basis of the 'usual' rate was justice. The basis of the employer's dealings with the short-time workers was mercy. So in this parable, mercy and justice meet. At, we must remember, harvest-time, that image of the 'end-time' of the

vines, that image of the people of God. And we are swept into
a dimension in which we find ourselves forced to face the
unpalatable fact that often in human society, 2,000 years ago as
now, our self-righteousness means that our sense of personal
value is enhanced, instead of diminished, by others not being
'made equal to us'.

For in both this parable and that of 'The Prodigal Son', Jesus
was astringently exposing the truth that, far from rejoicing at
mercy or generosity to others, we ourselves too often actually
feel devalued by it. Our sense of personal worth in the societies
we have created is somehow bound up with others not being
raised by an act of graciousness to be 'equal' with us. 'Are you
envious because I am generous?' the 'boss' asks. And the
answer, of course, is, sadly, a self-righteous 'yes'.

The God of these parables

And now we are in a position to reflect on what Jesus is telling
us of the nature of God and his dealings with us through these
tales which describe the conjunction of these two domains, the
one created by a stern human notion of 'fairness' and the other
by a larger rule of generosity. A conjunction which takes place,
moreover, in at least one of these stories, at 'harvest-time', i.e.,
the end-time of all things, the time of judgement. (And in the
other the celebratory banquet is also an image of the last times.)
For these stories are about divine grace and the necessity in the
very nature of God to grant it. ('But you are the same Lord,
whose nature is always to have mercy' some of us pray regularly at the Eucharist.) Not negotiated human rights, but the
truth that God, because he is the kind of God he is, meets
human shortfall with his own overflow of rich loving kindness.

But when no human shortfall is acknowledged, when the
chief sense is of duty having been done and the 'contract' kept,
then there is no aptitude to receive grace. For then we have
shut the door on that amazing divine domain revealed in similitude, and instead are insisting on dwelling firmly within the
small metonymic world of human perceptions of 'justice'. Jesus
is suggesting that we shall not find ourselves 'at home' in the
economy of heaven, shall not relish the heavenly banquet at
our heavenly Father's table, if our pleasure in sharing it is

untinged by any feeling for those others who do not. That is a spiritual mindset which will leave us uneasy and bewildered and even angry with the judgements of the God of the feast and the vineyard.

The rewards of the faithful?

Grace of this kind is not comprehensible in our terms. We are tempted to ask whether, in the light of these parables, it is worth being loyally virtuous and obedient? Is not too little account taken of the labours of faith? It is the very question Paul was to formulate for the Church, faced with this apparent anomaly: 'What then are we to say? Should we continue in sin in order that grace may abound? By no means! How can we who died to sin go on living in it?' (Rom. 6:1, 2). And this latter sentence is an appropriate gloss on the father's words to the elder brother: 'Son, you are always with me, and all that is mine is yours.' We begin to see an answer to the fears that these two parables engender in us, that divine grace is too unaccountable for us to risk. For two aspects of the question begin to emerge. First, that these two parables are basically not about the virtuous, but about the kind of God he shows himself to be in his dealings with the outcasts. For his dealings with his faithful ones we must look for more focused teaching in other parables.

But, second, there is nevertheless some indication here of how Jesus wanted us to understand the extraordinarily inclusive way in which God views the potential of his faithful followers. It is as beings who by their obedient loyalty can, if they are willing, become assimilated to him and his domain so that they instinctively think as he thinks and judge as he judges – with mercy, with generosity. They *are not in competition with the outcasts*, but potentially fellow-workers with God for a good which, to be fully achieved, must include those on the margins. (The Good Samaritan story had this at its heart.) They are a part of his action ('Son, you are ever with me') and their rewards are not to be seen as doled out meagrely but as a full participation in the riches of heaven ('and all that I have is yours'). For the full-time workers their contract was quite safe, meeting their agreed due. The point is surely that in God's domain nothing more than one's 'due' is needed, for that is all one could require. It is a sign of that sufficiency of provision for the faithful which is secured by the justice of the divine contract. To demand more must be to acknowledge a need for mercy.

And, of course, that acknowledgement of the need for mercy in the light of God's sovereignty was what so many of Christ's parables sought to inspire. The demand for it, implicit and explicit, was, conversely, what roused the greatest anger against him in so many of those who saw in themselves no need of it. For 'self-righteousness', in so many of these stories, is the enemy of grace. There are a number of shorter parables – what one might call micro-parables – which cluster round this theme, and so can be seen in relation to these two major parables we have just looked at: with the emphasis on the lavish provision by the Sovereign God of care for the outcast, the lost, the wanderer. It is to those we must now turn.

5 The Parables of 'The Lost Sheep', 'The Pharisee and the Tax-Gatherer', 'The Lost Coin', 'The Two Debtors' and 'The Servant's Reward'

'The Lost Sheep' (Matt. 18:12–14; Luke 15:4–7)

This story, again one of Christ's best known, is recounted in both Luke and Matthew's gospels, each gospel-writer emphasising a different aspect of its single overall theological meaning. We have already seen that it was, with the stories of 'The Lost Coin' and 'The Prodigal Son', in Luke's gospel one of the three stories Jesus tells in response to the criticism that he 'welcomes sinners and eats with them'. In this context, the comment given at the end of the story of 'The Lost Coin' meshes with both the other stories and directly confronts the criticism made of Jesus by the Pharisees: 'Just so, I tell you, there will be more joy in heaven over one sinner who repents than over ninety-nine righteous persons who need no repentance.'

A comparison of contexts

Seemingly by contrast, Matthew embeds the story in discussion between Jesus and his disciples about 'the greatest in the Kingdom of heaven'. The contrast is only apparent, not real. For Luke's account of the same discussion indicates it had a personal element (Luke 9:46): the disciples were arguing among themselves 'as to which of *them* was the greatest' (italics my own). Mark's account is even more pointed (Mark 9:33–35). After a journey, they have arrived at their destination (a house in Capernaum) and there Jesus asks them what they were discussing on the way. The detail that follows is delightful in its truthfulness: 'But they were silent.' *They don't want to tell him.* Why? Because they have already learned enough of him to be uneasily rather ashamed of the subject of their discussion: 'For on the way they had discussed with one another who was the greatest' (RSV).

In each account of this incident, Mark's, Luke's and

Matthew's, Jesus' response is the same. He calls a child and puts
him among them and warns them, in Matthew's words, 'Unless
you turn and become like children, you will never enter the
kingdom of heaven. Whoever humbles himself like this child,
he is the greatest in the kingdom of heaven' (Matt. 18:3–4, RSV).
Mark's version of this is 'If anyone would be first, he must be
last of all and servant of all' (9:35, RSV); and Luke's: 'He who
is least among you all is the one who is great' (9:48, RSV).

All three accounts, significantly, then go on to speak of
'receiving' such a child. Matthew's account describes Jesus
insisting 'whoever receives one such child in my name receives
me'. Mark and Luke add to this, 'and whoever receives me,
receives not me but him who sent me'. So the issue of 'recep-
tion', of 'acceptance', is crucial here to the notion of status in
the Kingdom which is God's. To have 'status' in God's domain
is somehow linked with fully accepting those who are themselves 'lowly', and thus in themselves 'signs' of the nature of
the Kingdom of heaven and the God who rules that heaven.
Hence Matthew's account continues with a sharp warning:
'Take care that you do not despise one of these little ones.' (In
Mark this reads, 'If any of you put a stumbling block before
one of these little ones who believe in me, it would be better
for you if a great millstone were hung around your neck and
you were thrown into the sea.')

And it is from this severe warning not to despise the childlike,
the least important, that the story, in Matthew, of 'The Lost
Sheep' grows. In one sense it sits uneasily with the foregoing,
and one can see why the introductory clause 'For the Son of
Man came to save the lost' appears in a number of ancient
authorities. But at a deeper level there is coherence here: for
the double theme has been introduced, first, of heavenly greatness being best expressed in such human terms as humbleness,
vulnerability, lowliness – all inherent both in the child's contemporary social position and in the childlike state. And the second
theme is of the profound value set by God on those whom
the world views dismissively. Seen from this perspective, the
comment at the end of Luke's version of the parable, about
'joy in heaven over one sinner who repents', converges with
that at the end of Matthew's version: 'So it is not the will of
your Father in heaven that one of these little ones should be
lost.'

Aptitude for, greatness within, the Kingdom of heaven, is thus not a matter of prescription, of maintaining certain formal practices however worthy or good, whether in codified social or formal religious behaviour. In their different ways both gospel writers propose this by the context they give the story; though traditionally Matthew's version has been seen as directed at the way the early Church's leaders cared for those they were shepherding who might be adrift.

St Luke's emphasis

The contemptuous note of the Pharisees' criticism – 'this fellow' welcomes and eats with sinners – is understandable in the contemporary context. It is because Jesus is seen as a leader of an emerging religious movement that he will be judged by what to the Pharisees are the right standards of such a leader in the Kingdom of God, that is, the highest and most astringent patterns of behaviour in accordance with the Law given by God. It would seem obvious that this involves avoiding bad company. Such 'bad company' included those who by their profession or life-style excluded *themselves* from social inter-course with upright men and women – tax-collectors and prostitutes, for instance. It would also include any who were ritually unclean like the woman whose flux had for twelve years made her a social pariah, or like those who had touched a corpse or even a leper. And it would include any who by a wilful act of wrong had set themselves apart from 'the right-eous', and who had not expressed penitence.

We need to recognise that there was in contemporary religious thinking no bar to repentance, and the Pharisees along with most other Jewish religious groups would deem a man acceptable to God and therefore themselves if he had admitted wrong and expressed penitence. So the chasm that existed between their understanding and that which Jesus expressed was the worth of that man or woman directly outside the pale *even before any signs of penitence* had been confirmed. Now the radical nature of the God Jesus declared becomes clear. The one who is the outcast, the one who is 'lost' is in this Lucan account of the story of profound value to God – value equal to those safely with the shepherd. In both this story and that of 'The Prodigal Son' Luke emphasises Jesus' account of the *tenderness* of the God who searches out the lost: for instance, the detail, only in Luke, of the shepherd having found the lost sheep, laying it on his shoulders to bring it home. This remains even today the way Middle Eastern shepherds carry home an animal injured, sick or exhausted, which cannot itself sustain the journey.

So we are given a double focus in Luke's setting of this parable. First that God values those astray and goes out to seek them before there is any sign of the lost one turning towards home. *Therefore*, the implication was, if God so values them, ought not their fellow humans? There is no place, that is, for dismissiveness in the hearts of any who would make God's Law their own, their heart's rule.

But second, since such dismissiveness has no place in the demesnes of heaven, it cannot be applied to 'this fellow', Jesus, either. If he is 'outside the pale' of prescribed behaviour, then, if God is the God he describes, contempt towards him and rejection of him has no proper place in those who would truly follow God.

St Matthew's emphasis

We have seen that Matthew's version of the story is embedded in themes of what makes for 'greatness' in the Kingdom of heaven, and in receiving and accepting 'these little ones'. 'Little ones' is a term used not only of children but of the weaker or less important or more vulnerable or more lowly of God's people. The story therefore *begins* with the warning against 'contempt', against despising those who would seem naturally to draw despite upon themselves. The flock in Matthew's version is moderate-sized; one hundred sheep was average for a single shepherd to manage. Luke's sheep were left 'in the wilderness', Matthew's 'on the mountains'. Both give us a local context, a familiar landscape.

Both, too, put an emphasis on the 'rejoicing' of the shepherd when he finds the lost sheep. Luke (characteristically) expands this into a party with the neighbours on the shepherd's return. Matthew expands it in another way, using what appears as the final comment in Luke's account – joy in heaven over one sinner who repents more than over ninety-nine just people who need no repentance – and relocating it within the metaphor which is the parable. For *his* shepherd 'rejoices over it more than over the ninety-nine that never went astray'. This leaves the way open in Matthew's gospel to draw out a further point, which is a challenge to all who carry responsibility under God in 'the Kingdom' (beginning, one must presume, with the earliest disciples): that it is not God's will (the Father in heaven) that any of the 'little ones' – the vulnerable, lowly ones of the Kingdom – should be lost. No such things as 'acceptable downsizing' here. Every soul matters. Even the ones who don't seem to. Therefore none – backsliders, outsiders – can be written off. Quite the reverse.

The reading of the parable of 'The Lost Sheep'

So we are now in a position to look at how this parable actually works as a metaphor for the processes of God's grace. There are significant differences between the uses of metonymy and metaphor in the two versions, as we shall see. Nevertheless, a common pattern emerges very clearly. The flock of sheep is owner-cared for, i.e., not tended by a 'hireling'. (Compare John 10:12, 13.) The owner-shepherd knows his sheep individually. Though there are a hundred of them he can identify one missing. (They would be counted nightly into the safety of the fold.) They are at graze 'on the mountain' (Matthew) or 'in the wilderness' (Luke). (These could indeed be the same terrain.) In either case it is dangerous territory. All this is the metonymic pattern, coherent and detailed: no disjunction in the picture. This is an agrarian economy, sheep are wealth.

But now we find the crossover between the one world and the other. 'Metaphor' begins to work. For if sound economy were the *only* principle at work, a shepherd would think twice about leaving virtually the whole of his flock in what is dangerous country, only to look for a single one who is missing. Some principle other than sound economy is therefore operative. Jesus is doing here what he does elsewhere: pointing to those generous or self-sacrificing patterns in human behaviour which are not wholly consistent with the tightly prudent behavioural framework society creates for itself ('The Good Samaritan' was an excellent example of this). And he uses these as crossover points, 'selecting' them as ways into the similitude of the larger grace-filled dimension which is *God's* 'society', *God's* 'kingdom'.

For what emerges in both accounts of the parable is that dominant in the life of heaven is the overcoming of the horror of 'lostness', being astray, being lost, 'losing one's place where one belongs'. These are seen as so dreadful, so inimical to the life of heaven, so overwhelmingly destructive, that the Lord of heaven cannot but confront them, deal with them, as the overriding principle in what he does. For 'it is not the will of your Father that any . . . should be lost'. And the 'kingdom of heaven' is, of course, but the expression of the will of God in the lives and being of his creatures. So heaven to be heaven cannot rest easy when there is 'lostness', or 'abandonment', and the Lord of heaven will therefore take the most costly risks to restore the lost. Being 'found' by the shepherd is for the lost creature the equivalent of the wayward son's 'coming to himself' and turning 'toward' his home; and his father running to meet him is the corollary of this. While his gathering him to himself, robing him, putting the ring on his finger, is the equivalent of the shepherd's laying of the weary, newly found sheep across his shoulders and carrying him. 'Rejoicing' follows, *because lostness has been defeated.*

We have to take seriously the force of the metaphor. Jesus is insisting that the nature of God is such that even the humblest and weakest creature being astray, being lost to him, is of the profoundest import. Delight in those who are safely within the Kingdom cannot be savoured without shadow while even one such 'little one' remains adrift. That is, yet again, it is the gathering in of the lost as of paramount importance to our Heavenly Father which is the very nub of what Jesus has to tell us about God. The joy and celebrating in the story, when the lost is found, is simply a confirmation of this. For this is a story – as with 'The Prodigal Son' – of a death defeated and a life restored.

The Father's 'will' is 'life'
And since this joy and celebration is in Luke's version *corporate*, the implication is that for all those who belong in the Kingdom of heaven, i.e. who express in their being and their lives the Father's will, the gathering of the lost must be *for them too* of paramount importance. Belonging within heaven means sharing the anguish of the Shepherd and the Father, without which it is not possible to share his joy. For those who love God, therefore, to see dereliction of the humble, the 'little ones',

is to see 'death', and to work for their restoration is to affirm that life which is the Father's will.

There are certain other differences in the accounts given in the two gospels which add extra richness to this micro-parable of grace. One is that in Matthew's version the sheep 'go astray'; in Luke's, the shepherd 'loses' his sheep. It is a significant variant for it means that in Luke's account, the shepherd takes ultimate responsibility for the wandering. For Matthew, the wandering is more clearly the choice of the wanderer.

Secondly, there is a significant difference in prepositions. Matthew writes of what happens 'if' the shepherd finds the sheep. Luke writes of 'when', describing the shepherd searching 'until he finds it'. So in Luke's version the metaphor discloses a shepherd God who takes ultimate responsibility, one who, whatever the risk, will quite certainly 'find' his sheep. *This* Shepherd, too, is given that touch of tenderness in carrying the wanderer home. What emerges from the story, therefore, is of a Being of responsible tenderness who will enable the lost one to do *what for itself it cannot do*: make the return journey. Such a picture of restoration is completed by the corporate rejoicing at the conclusion of the story, that feast which is the image of the end of time and the heavenly banquet – another detail here peculiar to Luke.

This brings us to a further point. For the hint of the End-Time in this metaphor must not be ignored. Therefore, while the story is of the present action of God, it is also about the nature of the End-Time experience. It tells us, that is, something vital about the Day of Reckoning: which is, that the Lord of the Judgement longs not for the harsh satisfaction of retribution, but for the recreating wonder of restoration: not for punishment, but for a life renewed. Hence the drama of divine energy searching out those astray to bring them, even when of themselves they are not able, into the orbit of their proper sphere. Here again, as with the 'Prodigal Son' parable, we have a little narrative which is parallel with the actual life and death of our Lord. When we come to the parables dealing more specifically with the Last Things it will be important to remember these pointers.

And this brings us back to the two gospel settings of the story. For in each case it is addressed to leaders (surely all leaders – leading citizens – not simply religious ones?); though in Matthew it is to the leaders among Jesus' own followers, and in Luke's towards the official religious leaders of the nation. In each case they have made a presumptuous 'judgement': a pre-empting of God's final Judgement by those who presume to make judgements on his behalf. Hence, in both versions, Jesus is attacking the judgemental pride of those who consider themselves righteous and are therefore daily holding – so to speak – a Court of the Last Judgement. The metaphor allows us to hold the human imposture against the divine reality – and be ashamed.

'The Pharisee and the Tax-Gatherer' (Luke 18:9–14)

The relation of the story of 'The Pharisee and the Tax-Gatherer' to the above is therefore immediate. Indeed Luke introduces it with a gloss which explicitly makes the connection: 'He also told this parable to some who trusted in themselves that they were righteous and regarded others with contempt' (Luke 18:9).

The setting of *prayer* is all-important here, taking us at once into the metaphoric mode of the parable For the two characters in the story express their view of themselves and of others *in God's presence*, as at his Judgement Throne, and *to* him. So the incident is a miniature interim Judgement Day. The conclusion of the story confirms this. *The issue is* (18:14) which of the two left the scene 'justified' (vindicated)? And the final comment, about the exalted being humbled and the humble exalted, is rooted in the vision of the 'setting right' of things wrong as at the Last Day. So now we can see how the metonymic and metaphoric patterns of the story illuminate each other and sharpen its meaning. The harmony and coherence of its metonymy, its integrated coherence of detail within a discrete world, must be stressed. All pious Jews were required, wherever they were, to pray twice a day. Those who were near the Temple at such times would go there. (Notice the accurate local detail about going 'up'.) We should note too, that the Pharisee's prayer was not as outrageously self-regarding as it sounds to our ears. He was praying by semi-formal rote, reviewing the obligations of the 'good' (= righteous) life his religion required of him, and thanking God that he was in fact more than adequately fulfilling them. One annual fast day was prescribed:

he fasted twice a week. He was required to pay tithes on the produce of his land. In fact he tithed on everything he possessed. (Like the difference today between tithing only on one's income after tax and tithing on gross income and on one's estate as well.) His way of life was comfortably respectable, not only in his personal life (he was 'not an adulterer'), but in the adequacy of his means. He had not been forced to resort to any shady way of making his living, as thief or conman – or even as that social outcast, the 'tax-gatherer' he could see at the edge of his vision as he prayed. So he is meeting his obligations, not only the basic ones but those austerely astringent ones set for themselves by that group, the Pharisees, who attempted to live every part of life in absolute obedience to the Law of Moses. A very high aim. He is a vivid characterisation of the completely 'good' man according to the observances of the Law of this religious nation. And thanking God for this way of life was an appropriate and right action: it was his 'sacrifice' of praise.

Given this picture of complete integrity and coherence, the *radical* nature of this story becomes much clearer. For this metonymy, this 'of a piece' picture is of the finest formal religious behaviour in this religious nation's life, unmarred by any apparent dissonant note. It is like the rich young man seeking to earn eternal life, who is indeed to appear a few verses later. If such a man is not 'justified', who can be? For whom do the delights of eternal life await, if not for such as he?

There is one tiny detail in this completely integrated picture which gives us pause. The story speaks of the Pharisee 'standing by himself' (RSV). (The Greek is a little ambiguous. Certainly he is 'standing' but the phrase translated 'by himself' is more precisely 'with himself' or 'to himself'.) So some translations attach this phrase to his praying so that the Pharisee prays 'to' or 'with' himself. The sting in the story would be accentuated by such a reading, but it is doubtful if this was intended. 'Standing by himself' would be an entirely proper position for such a man: it was normal to pray standing, 'lifting holy hands to heaven'. He would be speaking aloud – again as normal. There is, however, a sense of erectness, of confidence of bearing in the phrase; a kind of 'looking God in the eye without fear' – which goes with the sense of thankfulness for duty well done and a life properly lived. While there is nothing inappropriate here, the stance is 'pointed up' by the story and thereby adds to the sense of complacency. For if the words describe the behaviour of the man, the body-language reveals the heart.

Deliberately so, for the other character in the story – still within the metonymy, the coherent picture – prays from an altogether contrasting stance. So we are meant to see their body-language as deeply significant: indeed, it is one of the elements of crossover into the metaphoric mode. We need to be clear about who and what this character is within his little world before we can fully seize the importance of both his stance and his prayer. The Greek word here, usually translated as 'tax-collector', actually means a local customs officer. State taxes were collected by state officials, but the collection of local dues was sold off to the highest bidder, who therefore needed by whatever devious means to make himself a living by charging more than the official tariff. It was a form of 'business' inherently corrupting: it encouraged both harshness in the gathering of taxes, and fraud in setting them. So in the general view such local tax officials were seen as legitimised thieves. Consequently they were ostracised by 'decent' people, and had even lost their civil rights. Hence the point of the Pharisee's thanksgiving – that he has not been forced by penury to roguery or thieving or even customs-collecting, like this chap on the edge of the Temple courtyard.

On the edge. The tax-collector is hardly inside the Temple Court at all, but 'standing far off' makes his prayer. The word translated 'far off' is, while not precisely the same word, from the same root as the word used of the prodigal son when the father first sees him returning. And his stance is the reverse of 'erectness', and his prayer is neither of praise nor of thanksgiving, but an outburst of despair. As well it might be, for his case seems irredeemable. To 'redeem himself' according to the Law as stringently observed by that Pharisee praying up front, before him in the Temple Court, this man would first have to give up his present means of livelihood; then find out all those who had in any way been defrauded by him – an almost impossible task – and make full restitution to them, *plus* a fifth. No wonder that his body language is that of despair. The task of redemption is impossible. So he does not stand erect with hands uplifted, the classic pose of praise to God. Instead he stands in the posture of grief, despair and penitence, with

bowed head and with hands beating his breast. The words that
burst from his lips are pure petition, the petition of despair. But
they are also the opening words of Psalm 51, with the self-
defining phrase 'a sinner' added to them. The story has thus
placed him firmly into *his people's* history of going astray,
returning in penitence, and seeking forgiveness before the
Judgement seat of God: verse 4 of that Psalm runs:

> Against you, you alone, have I sinned,
>   and done what is evil in your sight,
> so that you are justified in your sentence
>   and blameless when you pass judgement.

The sense of this incident as a microcosm of Judgement Day is
thus strengthened. This man offers no 'sacrifice of praise', like
his fellow. Instead he offers what that same Psalm defines as
that which is pleasing God:

> My sacrifice, O God, is a broken spirit;
> a broken and contrite heart,
> O God, you will not despise.
>   (Ps. 51:17, NRSV marginal)

For the metaphoric mode of this parable, which takes us into
the transactions of divine Judgement as at the Last Day, takes
us also into the long history of this man's nation with their
God. The two men standing here typify the tensions of that
history: righteous obedience which so easily becomes self-
righteousness, and legalism and judgementalism which could
so easily lead to black despair, 'lostness' for ever. How shall
this be judged, on the Last Day? To the shock of his hearers,
Jesus declares the Judgement of God (and in so doing claims
implicitly the divine authority). The grieving sinner is 'vindicated', 'justified', *by God*: not by his fellows. It is 'justification' in
the sense that Paul was to use the term, supremely in Romans.
Nothing of the tight metonymy of vindication by religious Law
here, which the tax-collector had no hope of achieving; but
everything of the metaphor of grace which is the dimension of
heaven.

It is a shocking story, but only if we wish to limit the power
of God's generous grace – 'how *could* the man be seen as

vindicated?' – or if we wish to establish the credentials of righteousness primarily by reference to those who fall short of them; or, finally and perhaps most importantly, if we do not ourselves take seriously and feel horror at the 'lostness' of those marginalised, on the very edge of the Temple Court, who simply cannot, do not have the power, to set things right and thus walk confidently into the forefront of God's pleasure. It is this latter which most powerfully connects the metaphoric world of the Pharisee and the tax-gatherer with that of the prodigal son and the loving father, the short-time workers and the good employer, the lost sheep and the shepherd. Three other micro-parables reinforce this perception of the astounding dynamic of the grace of God. One is of 'The Lost Coin', a second that of 'The Two Debtors'. A third, which acts as a commentary on the elder brother in the story of 'The Prodigal Son', is that of 'The Servant's Reward'.

'The Lost Coin' (Luke 15:8–10)

This little tale is 'paired' with that of 'The Lost Sheep'. The one tale is of a man, the other of a woman, the one moderately well-circumstanced, the other very poor (the 'silver coins' described are often sewn into women's head-dressing as part of their dowry, and ten is a lowly number for such a purpose). So these parables are rooted in the everyday life and customs of Christ's contemporary world for both men and women.

How does this story 'work'? The metonymy is of a domestic interior, a poor home, which would be one-roomed and probably with no window. Hence the need for lighting the lamp (itself an expenditure). She will 'sweep the house' – this will be with a besom – because the coin is so tiny that all crevices have to be probed, and anyway the movement may cause the coin to tinkle or to reflect suddenly the glimmer of the lamp. 'When' she has found it (notice this detail of emphasis – Luke describes both the woman and the shepherd as searching *till they have found* the lost), then her relief and joy is such that she cannot contain it and she calls together friends and neighbours to share the moment of delight. The whole episode is then explicitly transferred into metaphor at the point of 'joy over restoration'. Suddenly we are in God's presence, in the courts of angels. (The name of God may not be used, or ascribed feelings, so that what we have here, as in the comment on the joy over the recovered lost sheep, is a circumlocution for the joy of God himself.)

We can go further. Neither sheep nor coins could initiate recovery so the emphasis of the metaphor is on the initiative of the seeker, the God who searches for the lost because it matters. This, together with the *intensity* of joy and the *priorities* of the activity – woman and shepherd do this *before anything else* – means that here is a radical, wholly different concept of redemption from that which the Law seemed to demand, which the sad tax-collector, for instance, knew he could never meet. Making impossible amends for past misdeeds is swept aside by the initiative of a caring God who himself takes the initiative and himself does the restoring. And again, 'present time' and 'the Last Days' are telescoped. For this is not only about the Day of Judgement but about God's very nature and therefore about his continuous redemptive activity. And not only about that redemptive continuum, but about the particular and unique divine initiative through Jesus himself. So it is, again, a little parable of the initiative of God in the life and death and Resurrection of Jesus. The metaphoric pattern is, yet again, of human disaster, divine rescuing initiative which is costly in energy and anguish, ultimate restoration and profound joy in circles wider than the lost one could ever have conceived.

'The Two Debtors' (Luke 7:40–43; cf. Matt. 26:6–13, Mark 14:3–9, John 12:1–8)

Only Luke recounts this parable; but the incident within which he places it appears in different forms in all four gospels. This setting is very important to the force of the parable, and we need to note it carefully. Luke places the story as being told in the context of a banquet at the house of one of the Pharisees where Jesus is a guest, and where an unnamed weeping woman, 'a sinner', washes his feet with her tears and anoints them with her perfumed ointment. Matthew and Mark each describe a similar incident as happening at a meal at the house of 'Simon the Leper', where Jesus' head is anointed. John places the incident in Bethany in the house of Lazarus 'who sat at

table with him' while Martha (characteristically) is behind the
scenes serving; and it is Mary – again characteristically – who
is named as the woman who anoints Jesus' feet with costly
perfumed oil.

There are certain elements these three other gospel accounts
of the incident have in common which can, I think, enrich for
us the meaning of the *parable* as we find it in the context Luke
gives it. First, in Matthew, Mark and John the story immediately
prefaces the Passion narrative. Second, amid the general disapproval of what is seen as 'excess' in the woman's actions,
Jesus himself accepts the gesture not merely with approval but
with warmth: 'She has done a beautiful thing to me' (Matthew/
Mark); 'Let her alone' (John). In each case, too, Jesus links the
action with an anointing for burial. (One of the charitable works
deemed most praiseworthy under the Law was to give the
friendless decent burial, and this included anointing the corpse
with perfumed oil.) Finally, in each case Judas is linked with
the incident, either – as in John – by voicing the disapproval
which Matthew and Mark describe as coming more generally
from the disciples (that this expensive jar of perfume, sold,
could have made a magnificent gift for the poor); or by his
going immediately from this incident to seek out the chief
priests, to discuss the betrayal.

So what is the effect when Luke takes such an incident (either
the same one, or one nearly identical) and, placing it much
earlier in Jesus' ministry, also places a key parable in its context?
In one sense one could argue for an element of stylisation. It
could be read as an 'acted out' parable, within which the story
is told as a gloss on the whole illustrative incident. To understand this, we need to clarify Luke's setting.

It is a formal occasion. Jesus has been invited to what is
clearly a banquet and the details indicate the formality. The
guests are reclining at table (v. 36), a Graeco-Roman posture
only used on formal occasions. Also the meal is taking place in
the public banqueting hall of the host. Family meals were eaten
in private, but formal occasions were traditionally public, so
that outsiders could stand round the walls or behind the
couches enjoying the conversation, and – if very poor – hope
for scraps from the tables. This meal must have been public for
a woman of the kind described to have entry.

Why has a *Pharisee* invited Jesus as a guest? We may guess

possible motivation from his inner musings as he watches the woman's behaviour to Jesus. It has seemed possible to him that this man might indeed be a prophet (he has invited him there as a 'teacher' (see v. 40b). But he is not sure. So, to be on the safe side, he has secured him as a guest, but not gone beyond the formal courtesies to personal warmth. Hence the reference by Jesus as to how he had been received. Jesus does not imply that his host has been actually rude. It was not always the custom on formal occasions either to wash the guest's feet or anoint him with perfumed oil: that would be the action of heightened hospitality, either an extreme of honouring or a family act. The assumption would be that the guest himself would have included these in his party preparations beforehand. For the guest's obligations were in the coherent world of this occasion as formal as the host's, and included ritual cleanliness.

So a formal banquet for a visiting teacher given by a host who is polite but privately doubtful. Some have inferred that Jesus had, prior to this, preached in the local synagogue, and the Pharisee, as was customary, was, as the important local man, entertaining the visiting preacher. An argument in favour of this prior action is that the woman is clearly in a state of great penitence and thankfulness in relation to Jesus: so something has happened prior to this which has moved her to this state of gratitude. Could it have been a sermon by Jesus which released her with a sense of forgiveness? Certainly there has been some previous interaction.

Whatever it was, the fact is that she has experienced some change, some turning point in her heart and life, and is overflowing with gratitude. To understand the force of this, we need to grasp that in Aramaic the word for 'thankfulness' is chiefly associated with the word for 'blessing' (in gratitude) or for 'loving' – the root is either *charis*, or *agape*. The word used here for the woman's emotion is *agape* – the word which was to become the name of the 'love-feast' Christ's followers were in the future to share.

Yet to the host at this table she retains her designation as 'a sinner', a woman of the city who is an outcast either because of her own way of life – prostitution? – or because of her husband's livelihood – e.g. tax-collecting? So by her very presence she is, for this zealously astringent law-keeper, an offence.

And because Jesus allows her to touch him he is colluding in this offence, since by that touch he has become ritually unclean, and thereby has not met the *formal* obligation of a guest.

All this lies behind the tension of the incident, and is the background to the questioning in the Pharisee's mind. This man *may* be a prophet, carrying with him therefore the holy spirit of discernment and the word from God. That is why he is being entertained. But far from observing the most astringent protocol, as a religious leader must be expected to do, he is not meeting even the most basic formal expectations of a guest. So the balance is coming down heavily against him. Since an ordinarily pious observer of the Law would never dream of allowing such a woman to touch him, it follows this 'teacher' cannot have discerned her character and therefore cannot be a true prophet.

The tension itself is therefore in the hidden agenda. How is Jesus to be characterised? Is he truly of God, or not? The banquet is the formal setting for a 'judgement' on this. And we remember again that 'banquet' is also used regularly as an image of the End-Time and the World to Come. Hence the sense of the 'stylising' of this incident. At the least one can argue that here Jesus uses an incident to 'act out' the same truth as the parable explores. Or – to put it another way – he uses the story to point up the truth of this encounter.

We must read the story against this tension. Jesus is meeting thought with thought, judgement with judgement. Jesus' opening words formalise this: 'I have something to say to you.' He is going to give an 'utterance', such as would be expected of a prophet. So his words will be assumed to have religious content, something to do with the Most High and his dealings with his nation.

What follows contains two literary devices: a proposed situation, and a question/dialogue arising from it. The sort of question which demands of the listener an inescapable answer. It is a *teaching* device, which specifically fits with the context we have already sketched out. Jesus is guest because he is 'teacher'; but to his host his *authority* as teacher is suspect. Jesus enables that authority to be established in his host's own terms, by formal teaching method.

And so to the story, tersely told. It is a familiar situation described, of a rich creditor with two debtors. They can neither of them pay him, so he writes off both debts. The twist to the story is that one owed 500 denarii, and the other only 50. A denarius was the usual day's wage for a labourer. So, allowing for Sabbath days, one owed almost two years' daily work (84 weeks), with nothing to live on meantime. The other owed seven weeks. That is the metonymy of the parable. A 'combination' of details which together make for a tightly inescapable disastrous situation. One man irretrievably in debt, beyond any hope even of paying. The other simply in difficulties.

But the word 'debt' is our crossover into the metaphoric mode. For in Jewish religious thoughts 'debt' is often used as a synonym for 'sin'. So now we are presented with the sort of picture we glimpsed with the tax-collector: two men being called to account by God, one of whom is beyond all possibility of reparation in terms of the Law; the other much less so. The *relative* burden of the two becomes in religious terms as it was in financial terms, a key issue in the story.

The other key issue is the generosity of the creditor. No reason is given for his act of great generosity: it is simply something he has willed to do, for which he has the freedom, authority and capacity. In that sense the forgiving of the debt is totally arbitrary. The result of no act on the part of either debtor, but simply the chosen response of the creditor to the need of his debtors. In the metaphoric mode this creditor is God, and his act of forgiveness is a response not to human making of amends, but to human need. The more desperate the need, the greater the generosity of response.

Hence the inescapable question by which the gospel writer achieves a double focus. For we are made by it to ponder both on what the story tells us about God, and at the same time to reflect on its implication for the incident within which the story has been told. Who 'loves' the generous creditor most? ('Love' as in 'overflowing gratitude' and 'blessing of a benefactor'.) Unavoidably, the one who has been forgiven most. And so the woman who is untouchable becomes the measure of thankful praise to God, rather than Simon, the strict observer of the law.

The metaphoric details reinforce this. Simon had given Jesus a formal welcome to the banquet, no more. But she had turned it into either a family occasion of intense joy, or a banquet of extreme honour, for she had undertaken the rituals appropriate to the more celebratory occasion – the personal washing of the feet, the kiss of greeting, the anointing with perfumed oil. She is therefore far more intimately 'at home' in the heavenly banquet than the rigorously law-abiding host. Lest there be any mistake, Jesus makes clear he knows all about the reality of her sin, the very genuine reasons for a society to find her untouchable: 'her sins, which are many . . .'. But her 'great love' places her within the orbit of heaven.

We can go a little further with this parable. For Jesus declares of the woman that her sins have been forgiven: and then – in the very role of the prophet which Simon his host had been testing – turns to the woman and gives absolution: 'Then he said to her, "Your sins are forgiven." ' Taking this back up into the parable which has deliberately paralleled the human situation in which he finds himself, this is a declaration of divinity. The creditor forgives debts, even the unpayable ones. God forgives sins, even the unamendable ones. Jesus, at this place and at this moment, forgives a woman's – irredeemable – sins. So the parable is not only about the nature of God which is always to have mercy, not only about the hope for the outcast, but also about the divine authority of Jesus, as he acts out the role of the divine creditor in a situation where his authority as teacher and prophet are specifically being put to the test.

Simon, the Pharisee, who has no sense of any great personal debt cancelled, may be assumed to be one of those who, 'at the tables with Jesus' began to say among themselves, 'Who is this who even forgives sins?' Now he is faced, through the parable and its sequence in the woman's forgiveness, with the authority not of a teacher, but of God himself.

'The Servant's Reward' (Luke 17:7–10)

This brings us to the last of the micro-parables on this theme. These stories of divine grace have as a counterpoint running through them the need for God's people to share the *perspective* of grace: to see the 'outsider' with the eyes of divine loving compassion, without needing to obtrude their own relative merit or to demand as their deserts a greater 'reward'. This final little tale addresses this last issue solely, belonging with this group therefore only because it relates to the elder brother, the full-time workers of the 'Good Employer', the Pharisee at prayer, the sheep and coins safely secure, and the lesser of the 'Two Debtors'. It glosses a little more fully what lies behind the comparison Jesus has made in the case of all these other figures.

The story appears only in Luke, and follows two pieces of teaching, one concerning the need to forgive repeatedly, the other to 'believe' with certainty. Both these are to do with attitudes of the heart, to God and to one's fellow human beings. They are the latitude and longitude of the life lived in 'the Kingdom', in God's domain. Hence the story, posited in the form of a question. 'Suppose you were a farmer.' A farmer in a small way, for he has only one slave. The details are combined quickly and vividly. That one slave therefore works in the fields in the day. When he comes in from them his duty – what he is *for* – is to wash, change, and serve at his master's table. After which he will get his own meal and rest.

So the question which follows posits an absurdity (we must remember this is a slave being spoken of, a possession of the master, bought for a purpose). Would you, as *master*, make an elaborate speech of thanks to the slave for doing what he is paid for? (Jesus is not speaking of ordinary courtesy, but of thanks given as for some extraordinary and unlooked-for service.) A rhetorical question, requiring the answer 'no'; and it completes the details which have been combined to make for a coherence.

The crossover into the metaphoric mode comes in the next phase, 'so you also' (v. 10). Again there is that disjunction. For suddenly the disciples are removed from the *master's* perspective and placed in the *slave's*: the shift throws a sharp light on the economy of heaven. Your perspective as slaves, servants of God, must be first to *do* all that is required of you by God your Lord; and then to perceive – here is the attitude of heart – that there is nothing *beyond the ordinary* about this, and, making an honest assessment, recognise that all you have done was what you *ought* to have done – what you are *for*. The self-assessment 'we are worthless slaves' does not mean the service is worthless or unvalued: it is in fact a Middle Eastern expression of modesty, but Jesus uses it as a sharp reminder of the truth of life. That in the scale of things humanity is under God's hand, and draws its value from being 'owned' by him, fulfilling his 'orders'. Taking credit for doing what one is created to do is an inappropriate mindset which can lead to future inappropriate and wrong perspectives, for instance on the 'worth' of others.

The relation of this to the parables we have looked at is clear. 'Carrying out God's orders' would be, for Jesus' religious contemporaries, observing the Law. Yet, Jesus insists, assuming merit for doing that was as inappropriate as a slave expecting fulsome thanks for doing what he had been purchased for. And far from coming closer to God as a result, such observers of the Law could drift further from him as little by little they became complacent, then self-righteous, then arrogant. All the time they had not recognised that the Law and the observing of it was but the external expression of what was truly required: a fundamental attitude of thankful and loving service by his people to their God.

It is this confusing of external with inward observance, and legalistic with creatively expansive service, which we shall be looking at in other parables by Jesus. Before we do so, we need to look at another group of parables by which Jesus describes further the nature of God and the Law of his domain. That is, the law in God's Kingdom of fruitfulness.

II: THE LAW OF INCREASE

6 The Parables of 'The Mustard Seed', 'The Yeast', 'The Seed Growing Secretly' and 'The Sower'

THE PARABLES WE HAVE so far looked at have at their heart God's generosity as the basis of his relationship with humanity. The grace of God is the very foundation of reality, the core of what Jesus came to declare about his Father.

Related to this is a second 'law' of God's domain: that of 'increase'. Jesus offers it, in four parables in particular, as 'the way the Kingdom works'. The micro-parables of 'The Mustard Seed', 'The Yeast', and 'The Seed Growing Secretly', and the longer story of 'The Sower', are all explicitly about it.

'The Mustard Seed' (Mark 4:30–32; Matt. 13:31; Luke 13:8), 'The Yeast' (Matt. 13:33; Luke 13:20) and 'The Seed Growing Secretly' (Mark 4:26–29)

The context
The parable of 'The Mustard Seed' is recorded in the gospels of Mark, Matthew and Luke, and its parallel, the parable of 'The Yeast', is found in Matthew and Luke, while only Mark records the parallel parable of 'The Seed Growing Secretly'. Mark and Matthew include the stories as part of Jesus' teaching 'by the lake', and both of them include in this section the parable of 'The Sower'. Luke places the two micro-parables in a different setting, immediately after his account of Jesus healing the crippled woman on the Sabbath day, to critical reaction from some of those present.

The teaching in which Matthew and Mark embed the story includes passages about Jesus' way of using parables as a form of teaching linked with the lack of understanding of the crowds. In Mark's version this becomes the purpose of using 'parables': that real understanding of the secret things Jesus was declaring was for his small band of initiates alone, for he was dealing,

like the prophets, like the apocalyptic writers, like the St John
of the Revelation, with sacred mysteries. Matthew's emphasis
is slightly different, suggesting that because the crowds do not
understand, therefore he speaks to them in parables. This could
mean either that he uses the picture language of parables as a
way of helping the non-understanding to glimpse truth: or
(remembering that the Hebrew senses of the word 'parable'
can include 'enigma or riddle') that what he said was to the
crowds – though he did not purpose it as such – a series of
'riddles', of enigmatic statements, because they were not tuned
in to the 'secrets of the Kingdom' (Matt. 13:11; Mark 4:10).

Mystery

The importance of this for our reading of the three micro-
parables is the emphasis on 'mystery'. For in each of the three
parables the actual crossover, from the very realistic metonymically detailed Palestinian world into the metaphoric mode
describing the realities of God's domain, begins from the fact
of 'mystery' common to all three of them. For 'the Kingdom of
heaven is like' neither the pinhead-sized mustard seed nor the
great tree which grows from it, but *like the way in which the one
becomes, extraordinarily, the other*. Similarly, the Kingdom of
heaven is like neither the yeast nor the bread, but the mysterious way in which the one transforms the dough into the
other. And in the 'Seed Growing Secretly', the routine ordinariness of the life of the farmer who would sleep and rise night
and day is contrasted with the mysterious secret work going
on meanwhile under the soil, which transforms the seed planted
months ago into a rich field of grain.

The fact that, in our world, these natural processes are now
identified and analysed does not inhibit this aspect of these
parables. For even to us processes are none the less marvellous
and serious for being classified: indeed, properly, our wonder
is enhanced. So to read these parables rightly we need to grasp
first of all the contrast between the *familiar*, that which is a part
of the everyday scene, and the *mystery* underlying it. Everyone
among Jesus' hearers will have seen tiny mustard seeds, no
larger than a pinhead: they are as familiar as the great bushes
which grew out from them, around Galilee, up to six feet high.
They are an ordinary part of the natural world beyond the little
houses. And within the little houses everyone will have seen –

probably daily – bread being made: will have seen the dough, and the twist of yeast, and what together they became. And between the little houses and the rough ground where the mustard tree grows they will have seen the farmers planting their fields in the bare soil, watched the seasons change as night and day follow each other, and admired the fields gold at harvest time. All this in every detail is *ordinary*, part of their familiar metonymic world.

Yet the parables each urge the mystery of God's work behind the ordinary. It is not only in the astonishing contrast between the two stages in each parable. It is that even *while life is proceeding* so familiarly, something tremendous is going on. To grasp the dimensions of the mystery which Jesus is suggesting as 'of the nature of the Kingdom of heaven', we must remember that elsewhere the 'seed' is a symbol of new life out of death, of resurrection. It is so in Jewish tradition; it is so in church writing – for instance Paul uses it in 1 Corinthians 15, and St John in the gospel (John 12). The metaphoric mode of the parable is suggesting that God's domain has the astonishingly mysterious quality, *within our familiar world*, that for instance pertains to the transforming new life which comes from the death of the seed, deep in the soil. That God's domain permeates wholly and mysteriously our everyday life as the yeast does which becomes one with the bread it creates. That while we go about the ordinariness of our daily living miraculous things are happening 'in the fields' all around us; on which our prosperity, indeed our very survival, depends.

Dynamic

This leads us into another truth of 'the way the Kingdom works' which the metaphoric mode of these three parables suggests. That is, there is nothing static about it. Jesus is indicating here what emerges with a slightly different emphasis elsewhere, that in God's domain there is increasingly energy at work, there is a dynamic which moves situations and people forward, 'unresting, unhastening, and silent as light'. If something happens – as the seed becomes a tree, the yeasty dough bread, the bare fields a harvest – then *some force is making it happen*. It is not simply an instant transformation, but a something at work upon something else with the power, the energy, to *change* things.

Two aspects of this 'energy' are implicit in the stories. One is that its operation demands patience. Due process takes due time. In the context Jesus is telling the parables, he could be warning listeners that the great transformation of life for which they look from the coming Messiah will only be completed in the time it properly takes. The seed is not overnight a six-foot bush giving the birds of the air shelter. The yeast needs time to permeate the dough. The seed in the fields needs the cycle of seasons. The dynamic of God's domain is present and at work, but its full achievement is not yet. Therefore they must have the patience of faith in a God who is at work.

The second quality of this dynamic energy is the obverse of the first. If faith and patience are demanded while the mysterious force is at work, *nevertheless* that force is irresistible and what it will achieve, certain. There *will* be harvest; there *will* be bread; there *will* be great bushes, where before was only planting and dough and a microscopic seed.

And this brings us to the most important point of these micro-parables, to which the 'mystery' and the 'dynamic' are adjuncts. For the contrast on which these parables are built is both *qualitative* and *quantitive*. Something, in both their metonymic and their metaphoric modes, changes and becomes something else, something much more far-reaching. If we examine the nature of what we are presented with, it is not only of 'transformation' but of an astonishing 'increase'. The tiny seed has become so great a tree that it can be a home to the birds of the air. The tiny measure of yeast is mixed with (literally 'hidden in') three measures of flour and becomes the daily sustenance for a family. The 'seed scattered on the ground' sprouts (he does not know how) and becomes 'first the stalk, then the head, then the full grain in the head' (Mark 4:28).

Indeed, to press the point Jesus deliberately exaggerates: he uses with reference to the mustard tree phrases found in Ezekiel (31:6) and Daniel (4:12) which are part of the description of the mightiest of trees 'towering high above all the trees of the forest', and its 'top reached to heaven'. And by a nice inversion, he has taken an image which in the prophets was used for overweening worldly power, and transmuted it into a sign of that ultimate enlargement which is God's.

This brings us to Luke's placing of the two parables, 'The Mustard Seed' and 'The Yeast', immediately after a Sabbath healing. The woman has been bent double for eighteen years, a condition perceived in that culture as being in bondage to an evil spirit. When she appears as he is teaching in a synagogue one Sabbath, he heals her: i.e., in the eyes of the crowd, he exorcises the spirit. His action angers the leader of the synagogue, who sees it (in *one* sense rightly) as 'work', and there are six days on which this ought to be done. Jesus accuses him of hypocrisy, since all present 'loose' their beasts – ox or donkey – from their restraint in their stalls, each Sabbath, to go for water. The woman has been 'loosed' from 'the bondage of Satan', after eighteen long years: surely this 'daughter of Abraham' has as much claim on release as the animals have?

The comment with which Luke completes the account of this incident is that Jesus' opponents 'were shamed, and the entire crowd was rejoicing at all the wonderful things he was doing'. Immediately after this Luke places the telling of the two parables, linking them with the healing incident through the connective, 'therefore': 'He said therefore, "What is the Kingdom of God like?"'

So we are to look for Luke's understanding of these parables in the context first of healing, second of the defeat of the legalists, and third of the rejoicing of the entire crowd over 'all the glorious things happening through/by him'.

Clearly, therefore, the import of 'The Mustard Seed' and 'The Yeast' for Luke is of the mysterious power of God which gloriously frees, and transforms and increases the potential of life. But also there is an element (as is so often the case) of the 'acted parable' in Jesus' act of healing, not least in his use of it to confront the legalism which would restrict the free flow of the merciful power of God. There *are* no limits, he is urging, to the mysterious lifegiving work of God, and you may not prescribe them. For is not the Sabbath a right day for God's long-awaited confrontation with Satan, who holds people in bondage? 'Remember the Sabbath day, to keep it holy' – what could be more 'holy' than such an enactment in miniature of the Last Day and the defeat of Satan which was to come?

Harvest, and *'The Seed Growing Secretly'*
For this language of 'Satan' and 'bondage' takes us by metaphoric mode into the world of struggle between the powers of good and ill. Hence the parable of 'The Mustard Seed', and

of the feast which follows, look forward in Luke, as the healing incident does, to the Last Times and God's final defeat of Satan by that same mysterious power by which the dead seed is increased to a mighty tree, and the dough is wholly permeated by the yeast. The description of the crowd 'rejoicing at the wonderful things he was doing' is a foretaste of that 'setting right' of the End-Time, that 'Good Time Coming'. We are reminded of Christ's message in response to John the Baptist's inquiry from prison as to whether Jesus was the Coming One, the Messiah, he who was to usher in the Last Times and the glorious Kingdom. For answer Jesus describes how the blind see and the deaf hear and the lame walk: i.e., he was doing the 'wonderful things' which were the signs of the Kingdom. For the Law of God which is the divine gift to the nation is not, as the legalists would make it, a charter for restrictive practices, but a liberation into that state where divine justice and divine mercy meet.

For not only is 'harvest' a recognised symbol of the 'End-Time', linked also in Christ's mind with the Parousia, the Second Coming; but, lest we should miss the point, Mark has added to the little parable of 'The Seed Growing Secretly' words which echo Joel 3:13: 'But when the grain is ripe, at once he goes in with his sickle, because the harvest has come'. At this point the *mystery* of God's secret work in the Kingdom, its ceaseless energy, and its fruitful *increase*, are brought to the point of divine 'reaping'. The secret work of growth, which is of God, is to an appointed end, when God looks for the harvest fruits of the domain in which his power has been mysteriously at work.

Hence the challenge of the parables is to acknowledge the mysterious wonder of the active energy of God shaping and changing and increasing that among us upon which it works. Again we have a double focus, because the parables are about eternal truths and yet about a particular moment, that in which Jesus, telling the parables, is himself a sign of the hidden work of God whose transforming activity is there, could we but recognise it, in the Person addressing us. The verse which in Joel's prophecy follows that which Mark quotes reads 'Multitudes, multitudes in the valley of decision! For the day of the Lord is near in the valley of decision' (Joel 3:14).

And this leads us inevitably on to the parable of 'The Sower'.

The parable of 'The Sower' (Matt. 13:3–9 and 18–23; Mark 4:1–9 and 14–20; Luke 8:5–15)

For unlike the three micro-parables, this story is not a simple statement about the divine Law of 'increase' with its attendant mystery and energy, but a complex statement about that which is inimical to this Law, and frustrating of it. Indeed, it could be called 'The Parable of the Seed Which Does Not Thrive'. So in it we encounter, in both metonymic and metaphoric mode, not only the goodness of God who gives increase, but something of the mystery of its non-reception. We are initially face to face here with that which has grieved God's faithful ones from the beginning: how is it that though his Word comes to all, not all receive it? How is it that the many either show no sign of having heard what is made equally known to them, or, if they do seem to have heard it, do not live by it with any faithfulness? In other words, why does the world go its own way when God's address is to all? In one sense, that is, the story is about those very issues Genesis 3 describes: about things going awry in what should be an orderly and faithful creation.

In the context in which the story is told, of course, this would have an extra resonance: why, when Jesus preaches, do his words bear fruit in some people's lives and not in others? Why could the religious authorities not take to themselves his message, and yet his disciples could? By extension, the question stretches out to include his life, and his death, and his Resurrection. Why have these so embedded themselves in the lives of some that they have 'borne fruit a hundredfold' and yet been ignored or disparaged or dismissed by others? This parable of 'The Sower and the Seed' could therefore be heard as about that fundamental mystery, the non-reception of God's Word of grace and increase in Jesus Christ.

But the issues it deals with go even beyond that. For if they hark back to Genesis – why is God's lavishness frustrated in his creation? – they look forward also to Revelation and the Last Times. For the parable is like that of 'The Mustard Seed', 'The Yeast' and 'The Seed Growing Secretly', in that in its structure it is a two-stage story: an initial situation, and an end achievement. The story begins in the familiar agrarian world of Palestine with the preparatory acts of the farmer in sowing. It ends in the equally familiar world of harvesting, a rich ripe harvest. The details in both are accurate vivid, coherent: it is a metonymic picture. The mysterious energy described of the mustard seed and yeast has been at work giving extraordinary increase, 'increase' that operates at the metaphoric as well as the metonymic level. But – here is the profound addition – not all has fruited. The realistic truth of the metonymic picture is that not all seeds grow and flourish. The observable truth of the metaphoric mode is that not all lives 'bear fruit' as they should. So these will not be part of 'the harvest'. And we then remember that 'harvest' is language for the Last Times, as well as vivid description of an observable part of the creation we live in.

The language of death and life

This reading of the parable is strengthened when we recognise how vividly Jesus uses in it the language of death and life. The 'death' language has strong verbs like 'devoured' (or, in Luke, 'trampled'), 'scorched', 'withered', 'choked'. The 'life' language is of birth: 'brought forth', 'produced'. Behind this latter, as in the parable of 'The Seed Growing Secretly', is the mystery that the new life is present through the death of the seed, so that we are really speaking of 'resurrection'. The final harvest therefore, of the Last Times, with its celebration of life, is in the face of death as a known reality.

So we need to look at what Jesus has to say, through this parable, of the mystery of this death at work in the field of humanity which should properly be wholly displaying God's new life. Traditionally, based on the interpretation Mark, Matthew and Luke each report as given by Christ, the *metonymic* details of the story are interpreted as speaking *metaphorically* of individual responses to the Word. (Though the claim that this actually was Christ's own interpretation has been widely challenged because the idiom and language of these verses is markedly different.) For instance, the 'seeds fallen on the path and snatched by the birds' refer in this interpretation to the lives of those from whom Satan snatches away the Word as soon as it comes to them.

But what might this metaphor mean? Who is at risk, what makes them at risk, and what does it *mean* that 'Satan immediately comes and takes away the Word sown in them' (Mark 4:15)? Matthew glosses that this refers to anyone who 'hears the word of the Kingdom and does not understand it' (Matt. 13:19). Luke adds to Mark's version a different gloss, that 'the devil' takes away the word from their hearts, 'so that they may not believe and be saved'.

Perhaps we may better get a grip on this if we pause to consider the metonomyic details of the 'path' and the 'birds'. The path where these seeds have fallen has two qualities. It is a means of transit: and *therefore* it is trampled hard. So that when the metaphoric language of 'Satan' or 'the devil' is used, what we have to grasp is that *just* as the path is a place vulnerable to the snatching of the seeds by the birds, so *also* is that condition of life which is its spiritual equivalent vulnerable to the snatching away of the words of life. What is this condition? May it not be that the 'path' image is that of humankind, in perpetual transit between two places, in a sort of spiritual limbo? ' "How long will you go limping with two different opinions?" said Elijah to the people of Israel. "If the Lord is God, follow him; but if Baal, then follow him." *The people did not answer him a word*' (1 Kings 18:21). Here I think we are meant to grasp the grand concept not only of the individual heart's condition, but that of the whole people of God and therefore of those who should through them have been blessed and led to God, the rest of humanity.

What is implied in the silence of the people at Elijah's challenge is inherent also in the parable. The path is trampled, humanity's heart is hardened. Hence the seeds do not sink into the soil, the Word cannot penetrate, and those powers for evil which are inimical to God in our lives snatch it away. (The emphasis here is on supernatural evil forces, in contrast to the psychological and worldly pressures of the rocky soil and the 'thorns'.) If we put together the three synoptic gospel versions, then the picture in this instance of death at work in God's fair field of humanity is that because it is double-minded, humanity's sensitivity to God's address is lost, and understanding therefore fails. And at that point 'the Prince of the Power of the Air', the power of evil which implacably opposes God, will snatch away from humankind that Word which could create for it new life.

The 'rocky ground'

When we turn to the realistic detail of the 'rocky ground' we are again vividly in Palestine. Jesus is describing what all will have seen: the seeds which shot up rapidly but wither in the heat of the noonday sun, and die.

All three gospels record in the commentary on this part of the story that in so far as humanity is like such a withered crop it is 'because they have no root'. The importance of the root to a plant in a hot climate is that it is the channel of sustenance: it taps down to wherever moisture might be which will sustain the crop under the hot sun. Hence, in metaphoric mode, the lack of 'root' in humanity implies being cut off from its essential profound spiritual resources. Hence, however immediate and garish the life of the plant, it cannot be sustained.

The gospel writers, in the context of the early Church, applied this to those who 'in time of testing fall away' (Luke), the gloss given by Mark and Matthew to this 'time of testing' being 'trouble or persecution'. Certainly this is applicable. But in a wider sense may the metaphor not address the kind of febrile culture we ourselves live in, where the prosperity of our human harvest is indeed in very thin soil, and where we are not tapped in, as a civilisation, to those deepest spiritual resources which sustain when the heat is on? Part of the resonance of this parable is that the scorching *heat* is certain: it is as inevitable an element in our condition as the noonday sun is above the Palestinian fields. Moreover, when our roots go down deep, that same scorching sun is in fact a positive element in bringing the field to harvest. It is only when we live shallowly that the heat is a death threat to our souls instead of a severe blessing.

The thorns

With the thorns there is no problem about growth. It is *luxuriant*. And that is our key. This is good 'growing' soil, no rocks, no hard trampled earth. Again, a vivid micro-sketch of something seen by all who listened. A luxuriant patch of growth in which the thorns in among the wheat have gradually grown unchecked, gained the upper hand and slowly choked the true crop so that 'it yields nothing'.

This is a frighteningly powerful image. The commentaries in the three gospels all agree that the thorns are, in the metaphor, to do with obsession with worldly matters gradually so taking hold that no attention to the lively oracles of the Kingdom remains possible. Luke and Matthew both speak of these in terms of both 'cares' and riches or the 'lure of wealth'. Luke adds 'the pleasures of life' and perhaps most tellingly of all, Mark adds 'and the desire for other things'. We need to note the word 'cares', and recognise that the condition addressed may simply be the 'dailiness' of life which can totally absorb in its busyness so that our awareness of eternal realities is extinguished.

So in metaphoric mode we are looking at that capacity in humanity for self-indulgence which, unchecked, becomes rampant and drives out all else. Again the parable speaks to our condition. Taking it further, in the context of the 'Last Things', it means a humanity unfitted for the heavenly banquet because its tastes have become gross and its palate desensitised.

The good soil

It is at this point we come to the insistence on the wonder of the harvest's *increase* – Luke settles simply for a 'hundredfold', while Mark and Matthew both touch on the lesser but still amazing fruitfulness of sixtyfold and thirtyfold. There is a sharp contrast here, after all the foregoing reflection on death abroad in the field; suddenly we have abundance, and the implied joy and celebration that goes with it.

The commentaries in the gospels each interpret this fruitfulness and amazing increase in terms, first of all, of *hearing* the word. The importance of this is stressed by the sudden exclamation by Jesus at the end of the story; it is recorded by all three, that he 'called out' (Luke) 'Listen! If you have ears, listen.' That is – there is a sudden urgency in his manner – he challenges them to 'Pay attention!'

And here we are at the nub of the parable. For its roots back in Genesis and its extension forward to Revelation all connect with the same theme: 'hearing' God's word, or 'not listening to it' for whichever of the reasons the parable suggests. Hence the teaching in which the story is embedded, concerning the fact that Jesus teaches in parables because people hear but do not listen or listen but do not hear. There is, consequently, an anguish about this story. Just as Adam and Eve did not 'listen', so humanity has continued not to 'listen' ever since. When we remember who was telling the story, and how it (and he) was not heard, there is a double irony in it, and a terrible pain.

Mark glosses this need to 'hear the word' with the phrase 'and accepts it'; Matthew adds 'understands it' and 'bears fruit and yields, in one case a hundredfold, in another sixty, in another thirty'. Luke amplifies what is meant by 'hearing the word' even more fully: those who 'hold it fast in an honest and good heart and bear fruit in patient endurance'.

So the astonishing 'increase' of the crop in the Palestinian field is, in metaphoric mode, a potential for increase in fruitfulness of the spirit in humanity. It is nothing less than transformation we are speaking of here, with a recognition that there will be variety of 'increase' and not all will be expected to attain the same richness. May it not be that Jesus is speaking here, not just of the astonishing fruit that individual lives can bear when God is at work in them giving new life, but of transformed humanity, that 'multitude that no man can number'? And with that, we are back to the promise of the Last Times, when the sorrow of the mystery of death in the fields has been overcome by the greater mystery of the 'increase' available to all who choose the way of life.

This balance, of wastage on the one hand and increase of life on the other, runs through several other micro-parables. It is to these we must now turn.

7 The Parables of 'The Barren Fig-Tree', 'The Return of the Demon' and 'The Talents'

The offence of sterility

If 'increase', 'fruitfulness', is a law of God's domain, then refusing the potential of such increase is an offence against that law. What emerges from so many of Jesus' parables as well as from his direct teaching is that this is no arbitrary demand on the part of an autocratic God, but a warning that this is the nature of reality, the way things work, spiritual as well as physical. We therefore ignore it at our peril.

The three parables, 'The Barren Fig-Tree', 'The Return of the Demon', and the very well-known parable of 'The Talents', all explore this truth. Each of them is an image of *waste*: wasted soil and tending, in relation to the fig-tree. Wasted space in relation to the return of the demon. Wasted financial potential in relation to the silver talents. Common to these is the *cause* of waste: 'sterility'. And this is seen as alien to the Kingdom of God. The implication is clear: 'fruit, or be cut down'; 'steward resources, or lose them'; 'fill the emptiness of your life with good, or evil will take up squatters' rights.' But what in fact does this mean in the currency of everyday life? In Mark's gospel (4:24) a saying is added to the one which also appears concluding the parable of 'The Talents' in Matthew: 'To those who have, more will be given, but from those who have nothing, even what they have will be taken away'. The extra saying in Mark runs, 'The measure you give will be the measure you get . . .' That is the warning which in its profoundest sense Jesus is giving in these parables. In other words, we are ourselves responsible for the kind of spiritual sterility of which Jesus is speaking.

Time limits

In one sense the judgement on sterility is already present in the coming of the Teller of these tales (cf. John 9:39 'I came into this world for judgment so that those who do not see may see, and those who do see may become blind'). But the parables themselves, like the life and death of Jesus, speak of the enactment of the judgement as *deferred*, God for mercy's sake extending the period of grace which runs through this moment of pronouncement, before the judgement is put into effect. For the early Church this period of grace was seen as the time between the Incarnation and the Second Coming. In fact the gospels suggest something more complex, since the focus of the teaching and parables is on *both* individual and corporate amendment of life, with, therefore, a shifting time span.

What is emphatically clear in these three parables, as in the rest of Jesus' teaching, is that the time of grace does have a natural end. It is not entirely open. There *will* be a termination, though 'no one knows the day nor the time'. In the story of 'The Barren Fig Tree' this is expressed quite specifically: 'Sir, let it alone for one more year' (Luke 13:8). In the parable of 'The Talents' the time available is until the return of the master: an unpredictable period, but with a sure termination. In 'The Return of the Demon' the time span is more cyclic, with, nevertheless, the return of the evil spirit a sure event – part of 'the way things are' – after its sojourn in the desert.

Sterility; and time for renewal of fruiting, but a limited time, for 'the axe is at the root of the tree'. This is the overt theme of these parables. We need to look now at some of the profounder developments of this theme as the structure and context of the stories reveal it. Something of its richness is caught in the familiar lines of George Herbert:

> Who would have thought my shrivell'd heart
> Could have recover'd greenness? . . .

> These are thy wonders, Lord of power,
> Killing and quick'ning, bringing down to hell
> And up to heaven in an houre.

'The Barren Fig-Tree' (Luke 13:6–9)

(i) The setting

In Luke's arrangement of the material, Jesus is prompted to tell this story of the barren fig-tree by a discussion about a tragedy which was clearly topical at the time, but the details of which are now lost to us. This was the killing by the Roman governor of some men from Galilee, whilst they were making their ritual sacrifice. The injustice of this (or otherwise – were they inciting rebellion?) we do not know; and in any case it is not germane to the point of the incident as it was being discussed with Jesus by some of the crowd.

For clearly the issue for them is not of civil law but of *spiritual* offence: the gruesome incident has brought to the forefront – again – the issue of the relative 'righteousness' of some compared with others. For the crowd this is conceivably an example of God striking down, through the secular power of Rome, persons who were more sinful than their fellows. (Otherwise, this view runs, they would not have so suffered.)

Jesus challenges this view, with its inherent self-righteousness on the part of those watching others suffer. He takes another example of unexpected calamity, an accident when 'the tower of Siloam' fell, killing eighteen. Victims like this are *not* necessarily 'worse sinners' – he uses an emphatic 'No' twice. And in relation to each incident he turns the inquisition upon the crowd making their complacent judgement: 'No, I tell you; but unless *you* repent, you will all perish as they did' (Luke 13:3 and 4).

So, as in other parables we have looked at, the setting of the story of the barren fig-tree is of a strong rejection by Jesus of self-righteousness as a tenable religious position for his fellow Jews, and an insistence that their own need of repentance is as great as that of any other putative sinners. And that this need is urgent. So issues of justice and mercy, sin and repentance arise from reflecting on the mysterious nature of *calamity*.

(ii) The story

Thus when we come to the story itself, we already have a clue as to how the metaphoric mode will interact with the metonymic. The latter is vividly realised: the vineyard with other fruit trees planted among the vines, one of them a fig-tree. Like the seeds of another story, some trees bear fruit, others do not. The characters of the story are recognisable figures of the local landscape: the owner checking the productivity of his orchard, the gardener whom he employs to work within it. But here we suddenly find ourselves moving into metaphor. For at one level the owner's priority, that none of his precious soil should be wasted on a barren tree, is balanced against the gardener's priority, that no tree should be unnecessarily destroyed. It is the voice of one whose responsibility is to appraise and make right use of his domain, as against one whose whole life is spent in tending and nurturing. Hence we realise that at the metaphoric level *we are listening to Justice and Mercy in dialogue with each other*. The dialogue, in other words, reflects back to the listeners their easy dismissal of the supposed sinners in the light of the divine mercy they disregarded, as it engages with that divine justice of which God's chosen people were so sure. And then, by a twist, the implication becomes clear. This dialogue between Justice and Mercy is not about some 'outsiders', some who have put themselves beyond the Law: it is about a prized tree growing in a vineyard – the very symbol of Israel herself. The tension between the owner and the gardener, between Judgement delivered and Mercy staying the axe – this suddenly, as Jesus tells the story, becomes of acute relevance to the chosen people, the holy nation called by God. And thus to all since, including in our own day, who claim God's special care. From whom he has 'come looking for fruit' over an extended period, 'and still I find none'. (A fig-tree was given three years for its fruit to become clean before any crop could be expected from it, so the owner is speaking of a wait of *six* years. And since figs use a great deal of nourishment, it was taking out of the soil, from the vines, value which was not matched by any return. The symbolism, applied to an errant people, is very clear.)

'Mercy staying the axe'. One is irresistibly reminded of another dialogue between Justice and Mercy far back in the history of this people, also relating to a calamity, when Abraham pleaded with God for mercy on Sodom (Gen. 18:16–33), 'bargaining' energetically for its life. 'Mercy' is similarly energetic in this story. Justice agrees to give space for grace: it is a limited delay, and there is no question of simply 'waiting to see' if things will be better next year, and fruit appear. Rather, this is a severe mercy, which will 'dig round' the tree and 'put manure on it'. Fig-trees were never normally manured, so what is being suggested is that extraordinary measures are to be taken, with the ground round the tree disturbed so that new nourishment can reach the roots. If even such extraordinary measures fail in this last-chance season, then Mercy the gardener will acquiesce in the verdict of Justice. The tree is irredeemably sterile and must die.

The gardener

Inevitably there are questions about the figure of the gardener in the story, the mysterious interceder. Is he there simply to make the story more vivid? Or to give concrete and material form to the debate between Justice and Mercy (a debate to which we respond because it underlies most aspects of our lives, from political structures to personal relationships)? Or is there a more personal meaning here? For this dialogue is of course finally contained within the very Person of God, who is himself the locus in which Justice and Mercy ultimately meet: that is part of the definition of 'God'. So indeed it is possible that this figure can be read as that of Jesus himself, at work *within* the vineyard and, so to speak, speaking on its behalf. Some writers have suggested an analogy here with Jesus' intercession on behalf of Peter when 'Satan looks to sift him like wheat' (Luke 22:31, 32). (Some read this as a trial of all the disciples, and Jesus as interceding for them all, charging Peter when he has himself come through the trial to support his fellows.)

We can go a little further here. For we saw that Luke's recording of the story placed it after a discussion arising from the tragedy of 'the Galileans whose blood Pilate had mingled with their sacrifices' (13:1). This setting gives the parable a dimension additional to the way Jesus told it. For with hindsight the resonance of 'Pilate', and 'blood mingling with sacrifice' inevitably, whether or not intentionally, recalls the Crucifixion. So that we may not read the story without something of that profoundest mystery of calamity affecting our reading of it. Here indeed is the severest Mercy of all, and the profoundest stay of Justice.

> 'These are thy wonders, Lord of power,
> Killing and quick'ning, bringing down to hell
> And up to heaven in an houre.

'Supposing him to be the gardener' ... do we meet Christ in this parable?

Whether or not we do, his own urgency in telling it is quite clear. The holy nation, that Israel *of which the Church is the continuation*, is not bearing the fruit for which God looks. Its time is now short before it is concluded to be irredeemably sterile. Therefore the opportunity of this limited stay of divine justice must be seized, however severe the steps to achieve that.

We do not know the end of this story in its metaphoric mode, only the end of one of its chapters. Does the fig-tree bear fruit in the end, however tardily? The treble time focus of the parable – that of Jesus' own listeners, of the early Church, of humanity as a whole as its history comes to consummation – means that we know only a partial conclusion. In the end the fig-tree image addresses each of us as we grow in God's vineyard, whatever sort of tree we might be.

And the fruit? Certainly, of penitence for a sterile way of life. But penitence, to be real penitence, must issue in a changed heart and the life which issues from it. 'Doing the will of the Father' is the fruit for which Jesus looks. The next parable we shall read has more to say of that.

'The Return of the Demon' (Matt. 12:43–45; Luke 11:24–26)

'Either make the tree good, and its fruit good: or make the tree bad, and its fruit bad; for the tree is known by its fruit' (Matt. 12:33). These are words in a section of Jesus' teaching Matthew records as prior to the telling of the story of 'The Return of the Demon' (unclean spirit). At the very least, the implication runs, let there be fruit! The story of the empty house (as it could be called) 'swept', after its evil inhabitant has been evicted, and put in order – *and then left unused* – is a most vivid image of spiritual sterility, carrying with it a sharp warning as to the almost inevitable consequences.

The context
Matthew and Luke both record this story, embedded in a section of teaching by Jesus much of which Mark also records. In Matthew's account the parable is told immediately after some of the religious leaders had demanded a 'sign' from Jesus, using

the term 'teacher' to address him – hypocritically? What they are looking for, cynically, is evidence of his authority to teach. Challengingly, his response is to offer them 'no sign . . . except the sign of the prophet Jonah' (Matt. 12:39b). We need to probe a little into what is meant here. There is first, as Luke also notes, the implicit reminder to the religious leaders of God's holy nation, that the prophets such as Jonah were received in their own land largely with unbelief: but that Jonah was sent *to the Gentiles*, his message was heard and the city of Nineveh repented and turned around in its ways. 'Belief' caused penitence and penitence caused a new way of life. So for Nineveh the stay of grace meant that divine justice need not be punitively administered. Therefore at the Last Day the 'people of Nineveh' – Gentiles! – non-Jews! – would be a standing judgement against the holy nation of Israel, who had not known – as they had – how to hear the prophet of God and respond.

Similarly the Queen of Sheba – Gentile! – came 'from the ends of the earth' (12:42) to *listen* to the wisdom of Solomon. So she too at the Last Day will be a standing judgement against the holy nation of Israel, who had not known – as she had – how to hear the wisdom of God and respond.

This is harsh speech to the religious leaders of Israel. And equally tough when we allow it, today, to address a complacent and unselfcritical Church. But the greatest challenge is behind. For Jesus claims an authority 'greater than' that of the prophet; 'greater than' that of Solomon himself. This is going far beyond the Pharisees' demand for his teaching authority. What he is offering is an authority of 'Person', 'something greater' even than that of the prophet who speaks the words of God or the kingly wise man who thinks the thoughts of God. The claim is absolutely explicit, and challenges our own limited 'authorities' also. Matthew (though not Luke) underwrites this overwhelming claim with a reference to Christ's three days buried 'in the heart of the earth' prefigured by Jonah's three days and three nights in the belly of the sea-monster. It is the one who defeats Sheol who can claim an authority greater than the prophet or the king, the scientist or the moral philosopher. And therefore, again by implication, those who now come from among his listeners, to *hear* and *respond* to this One who is greater than Jonah and Solomon will, like Nineveh, like the Queen of the South, stand in judgement against the non-hearing religious leaders standing before Jesus now. As will those today outside our Church who respond to his word but not to the institutional Church where it has become sterile.

So the introduction to the parable in Matthew develops themes of judgement in the face of racial and religious complacency, and an astoundingly new authority, greater than any revered by the religious leaders, the authority of life over death.

Luke uses the same teaching material *after* the telling of the parable, but adds another 'judge' against these religious leaders prior to it, this time of their own race. For Luke's immediate introduction to the story is an account of a healing incident (recounted also elsewhere by Matthew), the 'casting out' of a 'demon that was mute'. Afterwards 'the dumb spoke'. Jesus' critics argued that he did such miracles by the power 'of Beelzebul', King of demons – while others 'to test him' continually clamoured for a sign. Jesus challenges the logic of the accusation that it was the power of evil which was being used to defeat evil; and then asks, if so, by what power 'their own' exorcists dealt with demon-possession? Let *them* 'be your judges'.

The detail that 'the dumb spoke' is significant here. For Christ's final comment on this incident and the argument that followed is, 'If it is by the finger of God that I cast out the demons, then the Kingdom of God has come to you' (Luke 11:20). Again we are reminded that 'the dumb speaking' is one of the Messianic signs of the presence of the Kingdom of heaven. So alongside the language in Matthew of extraordinary authority we can put this clear claim in Luke to be the Messiah, the Coming One announcing the rule of God.

Hence the material in both accounts introducing this parable opens up issues of struggle between powers which are extraordinary (Luke even includes the image here of the strong man being overcome by a stronger). The scope is worldwide – Jerusalem, Nineveh, the 'ends of the earth'; and other-worldly as well as this-worldly – Beelzebul, Satan, Messiah, demons and the powers to 'cast them out'. The power of life over death itself. And running through these are issues of the Last Day and Judgement: the bar at which humanity – all of us, nations of the world – shall answer.

We need to note one further detail about context. That is, Matthew's account rounds off the parable with the arrival of Jesus' mother and brothers 'while he was still speaking to the crowds'. Told of this, he uses their visit to point to the intimacies of the Kingdom of heaven whose authority he has just been claiming. The relationships of the Kingdom are 'family' relationships; 'pointing to his disciples' he says, 'Here are my mother and my brothers! For whoever does the will of my Father in heaven is my brother and sister and mother' (Matt. 12:49–50). Exactly the same point is made in Luke's account, where as Jesus is concluding the parable a woman in the crowd calls out 'Blessed is the womb that bore you and the breasts that nursed you'. Jesus responds, 'Blessed rather are those who hear the word of God and obey it!' (Luke 11:27–28).

So to the vast sweep of powers in this life and beyond, as context to this parable, is added 'connectedness', a glimpse of what makes, in God's domain, for relationships as intimate as family. How then may we read this story?

'The Empty House'

I have used this as an alternative title for 'The Return of the Demon', for the story is plainly not about the wandering spirit but about the person it invests. Jesus is of course drawing on contemporary perceptions of 'possession', but the dangers of removing an 'obsession' without replacing it with something as powerful are well recorded in our own psychological terms, so that the point he is making loses none of its power for us.

This is a parable where the metonymic and the metaphoric are fused, woven together rather than cutting across each other. The language of healing in Jesus' lifetime is largely a language of 'casting out' the demons. Therefore the image naturally follows of the space left empty. What is to happen to it? There follow two pictures; one wholly metonymic, of a house freed of a deeply undesirable and destructive tenant, where cleaning up has taken place and everything is 'swept' – all filth disposed of – and 'put in order'. Chaos has been overcome, everything is precisely and exactly as it should be. It is a house prepared for its next inhabitant, but no inhabitant has been invited.

The second picture uses language which is both metaphoric and, for Jesus' listeners, metonymic, for the wandering demon is a part of their culture, and his howling in the waterless regions can be heard in the desert winds. He is an integrated part of their world. Yet at the same time he is *beyond* their world, an inhabitant of worlds *beyond* this one as well as *within* this one, and to that extent he introduces the metaphoric mode in which 'likenesses' of the Kingdom of Beelzebul and of the Messiah, at war with each other, are glimpsed. Where is authority in this confrontation? With the stronger . . . with the One who has done the casting out . . .

But meantime the house of the person's spirit is empty and lifeless. Why? Because no relationship has been made, no new and good tenant invited in. How might this be done? How might it become a family home resonant with life and love? 'Blessed are those who hear the word of God and obey it': they are become brother and sister and mother. The house would then be inhabited with the intimacies of heaven.

But it is not. It is like the house of the sceptical religious leaders Jesus is challenging: orderly to the point of legalism, swept of any particle of the dust of even minor Law-breaking: and *empty*.

So when – as is inevitable – the wandering demon, restless in his desert, returns speculatively to his former abode, he finds it invitingly available. Again the language is both metonymic and metaphoric. For Jesus' listeners have, as they believe, seen this happen. It is part of their world. Will it happen to the dumb man whose 'mute demon' has just been cast out? May it be an element of warning to him, as to all those Jesus heals? But the metaphoric mode takes us further. For, as addressed to the religious leaders, it is a warning of the powers of hell, the real dangers pictured in the language of the evil kingdom of Beelzebul: that an empty religious structure will, even when purified, be surely taken over by evil if the family of God is not invited to dwell in it. If, that is, no heart is given to the religious edifice by active and loving obedience to the Father which creates the family home of God. Hence the picture of the 'seven other demons more evil' than the first ('seven' is a figure of 'completeness' – the full range of wickedness). Hence the final words of the parable have the force of Judgement. If the religious life of the nation has indeed been swept and put in order, as in the Pharisees' extreme puctiliousness in the Law, this will not of itself meet the demands of God. It will not, to refer to the previous parable, offer him the 'fruit' for which he looks. Only when the nation is bonded together as a family in loving and active obedience to the Word of God will the religious household be not only secure from the 'takeover' of evil, but offering God the fruitfulness and increase which is at the heart of the Law. For without it the house of the nation is sterile.

But of course the parable is alive and runs today. So how does it address *us*? As millennial Christians, does it not question us about the 'emptiness' of our spiritual house? Does it not ask the truth about our 'familial' relationship with each other, created by 'hearing' the Word of God and 'doing' it, and so becoming Christ's sister, brother, mother? Does it not test the quality of our 'fruit', our 'increase'? May it not be that it probes our risk concerning our so empty house, on which in our churches we spend so much time attempting to sweep out 'disorder' and 'mess' and have everything neat and tidy and regulated? Is not such a house at risk of tenancy by something worse than 'untidiness'? May it not be that *this* parable, too, is timely to our condition?

'The Talents' (Matt. 25:14–30; Luke 19:12–27)

The classic parable about 'increase' and the lack of it is, of course, that of 'The Talents'. By association with our own English word 'talent' we have tended to interpret this, popularly, as referring to our right stewardship of personal gifts, rather than any application of principles of market economy. In fact the story is more searching and challenging, individually and corporately, than either of those.

To begin with, we are talking, in Matthew's version, about such enormous amounts of money. A 'talent', as the note in the New Revised Standard Version of the Bible reminds us, was the equivalent of fifteen years' wages for a labourer. Hence *five* 'talents' was a lifetime's income. Luke's version – rendered in the same translation as 'pound' – was in fact a 'mina', the equivalent of three months' wages. It is the *rewards* which, in Luke's rather tangled account, are vast – whole cities, which would in fact equate with the vast sums of Matthew.

In other words, the scale is *huge*. And since any lost capital would be required from the unhappy servant's own means, this is a high-risk situation the parable is describing. We must keep this in our minds as we work through to the profounder meaning of this story.

The content

Matthew and Luke see quite different emphases in the tale.
For Matthew it is about Judgement Day and the account that
must then be rendered to God. So he places the story between
the parable of the girls running out of oil for their lamps as
they await the wedding procession, and the 'sheep and goats'
parable of the Great Tribunal on Judgement Day. It is the 'calling
to account' which is the theme for him, and heaven awaits the
fruitful servant who has made his charge increase: 'Enter into
the joy of your master' (Matt 25:21, 23); while hell awaits the
'wicked and lazy' servant who has made no such attempt:
'throw him into outer darkness, where there will be weeping
and gnashing of teeth' (25:30).

By contrast Luke places the story between the incident concerning Zacchaeus, with its glorious climax: 'Today salvation
has come to this house, for he too is a son of Abraham. For the
Son of Man came to seek out and to save the lost' (Luke
19:9–10), and the triumphal entry into Jerusalem with the
waving of palms and the acclamation of the crowd. So for Luke
the emphasis of the story is about salvation, and about the King
claiming his own. Its placing alongside the saving of Zacchaeus,
who as chief tax-collector of Jericho district could be said to
have a proven track record in multiplying money, means that
the parable is clearly not simply a paean to a market economy
as the ultimate value. And Luke certainly consciously links the
two, introducing the parable 'as they [the crowd] were listening
to' Jesus declaring the salvation of Zacchaeus (19:11).

But Luke gives also two specific reasons for the telling of the
story: (i) that they were nearing Jerusalem and (ii) because 'they
supposed that the Kingdom of God was to appear immediately'. So in some way the parable is to prepare them (the
disciples) both for the kingly entrance to Jerusalem (and
perhaps also for the terrible events to follow?), and also for the
seeming 'delay' in the overt appearance of the Kingdom. It is
therefore a 'road to Jerusalem' parable in both the literal and
the metaphoric sense, 'Jerusalem' the *heavenly* city being the
goal of all our life pilgrimages.

Luke also complicates the action of the parable by the introduction of what looks very like a different story as a secondary
plot. *His* 'master' is a nobleman going to a distant country to
get royal power for himself and then return. But after his depar-

ture his countrymen, who hate him, organise themselves and send a delegation after him, to say he is not wanted as their ruler. Some have paralleled this with an actual incident, when Archelaus went to Rome in 4 BC to be granted his throne by the Emperor, and was followed by a Jewish embassy to resist the appointment. They were disregarded, and on his return he took severe revenge. 'But as for those enemies of mine who did not want me to be King over them – bring them here and slaughter them in my presence' (Luke 19:27). The savagery of this ending to the parable, as well as being part of the cultural tradition, may therefore also refer to the actual revenge known to Jesus' listeners.

The story

We are given a clue, therefore, by the contexts Matthew and Luke each give the parable, as to how its two modes, metonymic and metaphoric, work together. Take the basic story unit first, that of servants charged by their departing master with responsibility for 'doing business' with proportions of his wealth till his return. (Luke in fact gives each of the servants the same sum, a 'mina' or pound; and there are ten servants involved, though only three report back. Matthew has only three servants, and they have varying sums 'each according to his ability' (25:15), five, two and one talent.) This basic story is coherent and realistically 'everyday', as much for us as for Jesus' first listeners. Wealth may not stand idle, it must be worked or it becomes sterile. So when its owner is not available to oversee this, he must arrange for someone else to do so. And he is likely to give them only that proportion which his judgement of their ability warrants, particularly if they are dealing with vast sums. For the cultural context from which Jesus is speaking, these financial stewards would be responsible for returning all the capital given them (making good any loss), and the profits also. Their own gain would be in the reward the returned owner would, in delight, accord their success.

So risk is involved, and reward dependent on the owner's appreciation of their efforts. Something therefore turns on the character and expectations of this owner. The two accounts agree in their version of his character as described by the *ineffective* servant: 'a harsh (exacting?) man', you 'take what you did not deposit' (Luke), 'gather where you did not scatter seed'

(Matthew) and 'reap what you did not sow' (both). We need to read the owner's response carefully. Its implication is *if* they know this to be the case, 'why then did you not put my money into the bank?' For then it would have gained its proper interest. That is, he does not in fact reject what is said of him as a distorted picture, but challenges the lazy and timid servant that even on the basis of such a version of his master (true or not), he acted illogically. Why did the servant fail? Timidity? – it was a risk to part with the money at all; laziness? – it would have taken time, thought and effort to 'do business' with the sum left in his charge. So for safety's sake in one version he 'buries it' (in Jesus' day the most widespread way of keeping treasure safe, and a practice continued across the world and down the centuries, even to today here in England for some anxious people). In the other version the servant is even more unsatisfactory, because he simply hides the mina in a piece of cloth.

The key to the tension between servant and master is perhaps in a phrase used by the servant in Matthew's version: 'Here you have what is yours'. The implication is that his stewardship laid him under no obligation to offer back to the owner anything other than that which was first put in his charge. But this is to disregard the nature of stewardship, which involves right use of time and opportunity, in the affairs of everyday life as in financial matters: that is his offence, and for it he will pay dearly. It is not for him to prescribe what belongs to his master.

The metaphoric mode
Pay dearly – and, in Matthew's version, eternally. For Matthew makes the metaphoric mode explicit by turning the rewards and punishments of the financial stewards into allocation of their eternal destiny – heaven or hell. Behind this lies the insistence that the Law of God's Kingdom is of 'increase'; and therefore 'heaven', that place of the future to be tasted in the present, is a place of fruitfulness, to be fitted for which one must oneself have learned to be fruitful. Similarly, the zone of hell is sterility, and its anguish, and that of those who find themselves there, is never to be fruitful.

But there is more, and Luke's version helps us towards it. For since the theme of 'salvation' is the introductory note of this story, the emphasis is on the servants who *did well*, as much as on the one who failed. If we take the 'sub-plot' of the second parable woven into the story, we find a master who on his return has kingly status and the right to confer authority over whole cities on those servants who have been fruitful – so that they become minor kings. (We are reminded of Jesus' promise to his disciples that in the Kingdom to come they will sit on thrones and judge the tribes of Israel.) But then the *nature* of this minor 'kingship' is immediately defined by the ensuing account of the entry into Jerusalem – on a donkey – and the events that followed. Hence, along with the insistence on fruitfulness as a necessary quality of conferred kingship there is an implication of that kingship's costliness – hinted at earlier in the 'risk' involved for each of these financial stewards.

Here, too, we find an acknowledgment of that same 'unfairness' we saw in the parable of 'The Good Employer'. The Law of 'increase' means that those who 'have' will be given even 'more'; those who are sterile will lose even what they began with – it will be 'taken away', for they cannot handle it. But the parable urges that there is no unfairness here, for the remedy is which is the servants' own hands: take risks, work with what has been entrusted to you: for it is *not your own* to leave idle. And if it is not your own, then you are guilty of theft if you take from its rightful owner the increase which *would* have been his had you done what you ought.

The parable obviously had local applications as Jesus told it, both to the religious leaders entrusted with the 'wealth' of God which is the people of Israel, and to Israel itself, entrusted with its special calling. But how does it speak to us today? Some would apply it ecologically, and there is validity in that: the notion of our offering back to God his created world made sterile, or developed fruitfully, depending on which sort of servant humanity chooses to be. But profounder even than that is the challenge to offer back to Christ – when he comes – 'ourselves, our souls and bodies', in a state either 'fruitful' or 'sterile'. Upon that, the parable suggests, depends whether we shall be in proper case 'to enter into the joy of the master'.

Parables of Right Humanness

I: KNOWING THE TIMES:
'THE READINESS IS ALL'

8 The Parables of 'The Budding Fig-Tree', 'The Doorkeeper', 'The Burglar', 'Going Before the Judge' and 'The Children in the Marketplace'

SO FAR WE HAVE been reading parables which are primarily about what God is 'like'. The emphasis of our next groups of parables follows from this. It is about 'right humanness', about what God looks for, as Jesus describes it, in his people. What is their right response 'like' to this God of grace and fruitfulness who has called them by name? In the parables, as also in his direct teaching and in his healing and signs of power, Jesus constantly lays stress on two aspects of what it is 'like' to be 'rightly human' in relation to God. The first characteristic is 'readiness', preparedness to recognise not only the signs of the times but the significant and unique figure in the midst of them. The second follows from this: it is 'obedience', the commitment of person and people to the truth perceived and to the One bringing that truth. The parables we are about to read explore this 'readiness' and this 'obedience' in a variety of ways, sometimes highlighting the joy and delight that attends 'right humanness', not only in the present but in the heaven to come; and sometimes spelling out starkly the consequences of 'wrong' humanness, when the truth is unrecognised or refused, and therefore the people concerned go the wrong way.

In this first little group of four parables there are two which emphasise the joy of humanity getting it right – 'The Budding Fig-Tree' and 'The Doorkeeper'. And two which warn of the dangers of getting it wrong – 'The Burglar' and 'Going Before the Judge'. We shall also look at a fifth – 'The Children in the Marketplace', which acts as a kind of commentary.

'The Budding Fig-Tree' (Mark 13:28f; Matt. 24:32f; Luke 21:29–31)

This little parable – it is really a micro-parable – has something of the tenderness of which we catch glimpses whenever Jesus is speaking of something delicate and lovely in the natural world – like lilies for instance. Here it is the first tender, fragile buds of spring. The story appears in all three of the synoptic gospels, and is embedded in all three in much the same section of material. In, that is, what has been called the 'little apocalypse': that section of Jesus' teaching which refers to the End-Time and what lies beyond.

There are one or two aspects of this context we need to take particular notice of as clues to our present reading of the parable. First, that those terrible events of which Jesus speaks as imminent – in the lifetime of his own generation – are a *mixture* of the dreadful but human in scale, and the terrible and supra-natural – the 'sun darkening', 'the powers in the heavens . . . shaken'. The first group of events are such as recur in human history tragically often – 'wars and rumours of wars', and a destruction of city and field, such that the great Temple itself will be sacked and destroyed.

The suddenness of the disaster is the suddenness of an invading army, from which the refugees will fly to the hills with no time to collect coats from home if they are on the flat-topped roof about their domestic chores: they must fly down the only staircase, an outside one, and *go*. And all this did indeed happen in AD 70, when the Romans after four years of Jewish revolt came and crushed it. Forty years after Jesus was speaking, so within his generation's lifetime.

But what have such things to do with a parable of *spring* coming? The clue is in that other category of terrible event, the kind of which Revelation and the Book of Daniel speak, the portents of the Last Things and the End-Time. For these supra-natural events, terrifying as they are, are the portents of justice and joy to come, and the establishment of the endless and unchallenged right of the God of grace and fruitfulness, of peace and delight. The too familiar horrors of human history, that is, must always be understood as in some way related to the long-term pattern of the apocalyptic battle between good and evil. Within it, even in the worst times, God's providence is at work, his purpose is working steadily to its consummation. That is why, immediately prior to the parable, each of the three gospels concludes the account of the terrible with the promise of the coming of the 'Son of Man', glorious, attended by messengers who will gather his loved and faithful ones 'from the four winds, from the ends of the earth to the ends of heaven': that is, from all the universes there are in time and space, including those (1 Thess. 4:16) which those long dead now inhabit.

It is profoundly mysterious and it is powerfully promising of joy. Which is why Luke's account interpolates immediately prior to the telling of the parable, 'Now when these things begin to take place, stand up and raise your heads, because your redemption is drawing near.'

The story

So, to the parable itself. In the realistic, metonymic mode of the story Jesus is describing – perhaps even physically pointing at? – one of the few deciduous trees familiar to his listeners in Palestine. Because deciduous trees are rare in his land, they are the more notable as signs of spring. For they are among those few which look wholly dead in winter.

And so this takes us at once into the metaphoric mode of the parable: as do trees in spring here in England, when, following the death of leaves in autumn and the enduring of a long, hard winter, we see, with joy and renewed wonder, the first green shoots of new life.

For this parable is about recognising that principle of renewed life in the face of death and horror which the Resurrection firmly underwrites, and which, it is the promise of God, will be the experience of all those who believe in him and love him, when the End-Time comes. It therefore says to us as we read it what it said first of all to those who heard it: that terrible things *will* happen, in human history and beyond; but among them will be signs, to those ready and prepared to recognise them, that God's summer is near. But for us, standing in the dark knowledge of that ultimate horror, the Cross (ultimate because there could be no greater horror than our killing of our Lord), and the brilliance of the power of the Resurrection which overcame that darkness, there is no excuse not to recognise the signs of new life, amid all the dark tribulations and portents which would shake us.

For the 'sign' of God's summer stood among his people
telling them stories to help them recognise him. It is the coming
of Christ which is the equivalent of that fig-tree 'putting forth
its leaves'. And it is the experience of Christ, for all of us who
have known him in the centuries which have followed, which
interprets for us even the disasters which we must face. So the
message of the parable is both reassuring and challenging: be
encouraged! The signs of God's endless summer are already
with you: *stay prepared*, therefore, to 'know the times' and what
they really mean. Stay prepared through your own experience
of the living Christ.

'The Doorkeeper' (Mark 13:34; Luke 12:35–38; see also Matt. 24:42)

The challenge implicit in the parable of 'The Budding Fig-Tree'
is made explicit in this little parable of 'The Doorkeeper'. In
Mark's account it actually follows directly the fig-tree story,
while in Luke it follows a passage of Jesus' teaching particularly
reassuring in its insistence on the certainty of God's care: 'Do
not be afraid, little flock, for it is your Father's good pleasure
to give you the Kingdom.' It is worth our looking a little more
closely at these contexts, because they help to mark the difference of emphasis in this story contrasted with two which follow
it in different accounts, 'The Burglar' and 'Going Before the
Judge'.

Mark's account moves from the parable of 'The Budding Fig-
Tree' to that of 'The Doorkeeper' by way of an admonition to
'stay alert' because only the Father – not even the Son – knows
when the moment of Judgement – 'The Day' – will come. In
the sense that 'Judgement' was *already* present in the person of
Jesus, this has a powerful irony, which becomes the sharper for
us reading it with not only the hindsight history has given, but
the experience of the living Christ with us as we read. For both
his first listeners and ourselves, however, the final consummation of the End-Time lies ahead, and so the injunction, which
'The Doorkeeper' parable illustrates, to be 'on the alert', applies
both to the *present* encounter with Christ and the *future* signs
of his Second Coming.

In Luke's account the emphasis in both context and story is

almost entirely of 'blessing'. The introductory verses are a series of statements about the providence of God for his creation – ravens, lilies, grasses – which amount to a song of praise of God and reassurance to Jesus' followers. So the injunctions which follow concern living this life as those sure in God of the life to come. 'Make purses for yourselves that do not wear out, an unfailing treasure in heaven where no thief comes near and no moth destroys.' Such a way of living is that of 'the Kingdom', like alert servants awaiting their master's return . . .

The story

There are quite significant differences between the versions of the story as we read it first in Mark and then in Luke. Mark's 'master' in the story is going on a journey (like the one in 'The Talents') while Luke's has gone to a wedding – clearly a big occasion which could last till the next dawn. Mark's 'master of the house' expects to be away long enough to apportion responsibilities to each servant, and to give the doorkeeper special charge to be on the watch: rather like a porter or beadle in one of our great hotels, or even like a security guard on duty by the door of a great house or bank. Clearly Luke's master of the house will not be away so long – but he will expect instant and alert admittance when he does come.

One version of the story, therefore, is emphasising that the return of the master may be long delayed: *nevertheless* the servants must remain faithfully alert and ready for the great moment of his return. The other version of the story, by contrast, is emphasising the suddenness and unexpectedness of the master's arrival, some time soon. Both are familiar aspects of 'waiting' in ordinary life, transmuted here into the spiritual disciplines of the life of faith.

But there is another marked difference between the two versions of the story, and that is in the development of what is almost a sub-plot in Luke's account, concerning the reward given to those servants whom the master finds alertly at their tasks when he comes back. For (Luke 12:37b) he will 'fasten his belt and have them sit down to eat, and he will come and serve them'.

Now this is extraordinary behaviour, a reward beyond all proper expectation; and so with it we move from the metonymic coherent ordinary world of servants with their proper duties, like security guards with theirs; and of employers giving them a pep talk about staying on the job properly while the boss is away, and the ticking away of the hours: evening, midnight, cockcrow, dawn – we move from this ordinary, recognisable world to something extraordinary. As though the managing director of the company, on finding the porter still faithfully on the job late at night, himself put on an overall, went to the canteen, seated the employee there, and then waited on him. With the added dimension that in the original parable we are talking not about employers and employees but about a master and slaves.

So we have moved firmly into the metaphoric mode. This is the language of God's domain, where 'wages' become 'blessing' (Luke 12:38). This picture of the master serving the servants – have *we* not already seen this (though not, yet, the disciples)? For Jesus 'took a towel, and girded himself, and washed their feet' before serving them at the Last Supper. And that *action* was but an acted-out parable to illustrate a word he had already given them: 'For who is the greater, the one who is at the table, or the one who serves? Is it not the one at the table? But I am among you as one who serves' (Luke 22:27; cf. Mark 10:44, 45). This is a standing challenge to the whole way of thinking of their contemporary religious leaders. It remains just as powerful a challenge to us in our churches today.

For here we are in another mode indeed, where ordinary values are reversed, and the faithful servant is served by the master. Where? At table, at a feast, at a *banquet*... It is the language of the End-Time again, the celebratory language of the great party in heaven which gathers in all, however humble, who have remained faithful at their posts: and there – oh, unimaginable! – they (we) are waited on by the one they (we) know as 'Lord'. Small wonder Peter cried out in protest! And that was only at an earthly supper. Herbert's lovely poem dramatises precisely the magnitude of the reality this parable of Jesus promises his faithful servants:

> Love bade me welcome: yet my soul drew back,
> > Guiltie of dust and sinne.
> But quick-ey'd Love, observing me grow slack
> > From my first entrance in,
> Drew nearer to me, sweetly questionning,

If I lack'd any thing.

A guest, I answer'd, worthy to be here:
　　Love said, You shall be he.
I the unkinde, ungratefull? Ah, my deare,
　　I cannot look on thee.
Love took my hand, and smiling did reply,
　　Who made the eyes but I?

Truth, Lord, but I have marr'd them: let my shame
　　Go where it doth deserve.
And know you not, sayes Love, who bore the blame?
　　My deare, then I will serve.
You must sit down, sayes Love, and taste my meat:
　　So I did sit and eat.

So the emphasis in this story of 'The Doorkeeper' as Luke tells it is entirely on the blessing which attends those who are 'ready', who are prepared, who have stayed faithful, and attentive to the signs of the times. Mark's version is sharper, with the hint of a warning that there is always a danger we shall nod off at the critical moment. Hence the reiterated, 'Keep awake!' What is in balance is the power and authority of the 'Son of Man' returning 'in glory' and his angels with him – unimaginable procession of transcendent splendour – and the Son of Man the disciples – and we – know and experience, who, in a variety of ways, humbly washes our feet and serves us at table. Only the metaphoric mode can catch the exactly equivalent truth of *both* these pictures of our Lord; for the same Lord who authoritatively and properly requires us to be alert in our service and quick to see the 'signs' of his presence, is the one who puts on a servant's utilitarian garb, and as *part of his relationship with us*, in delight, serves us.

'The Burglar' (Matt. 24:43; Luke 12:39)

In Matthew's gospel the parable of 'The Doorkeeper' has been reduced to the admonition, 'Keep awake, therefore, for you do not know at what hour your Lord is coming' (Matt. 24:42). This is followed, however, immediately, by the story which also succeeds the fully developed 'Doorkeeper' parable in Luke's account – the story of 'The Burglar'. And in *this* parable the emphasis has shifted to the price of inattentiveness, the appalling consequences that follow 'unreadiness'.

The key to understanding the emphasis of the metaphoric mode of this parable is perhaps in the context Matthew gives, of a reference to the days of Noah. For the point of the reference is not so much the alert faithfulness of Noah, who discerned the times and prepared the Ark accordingly – though certainly this is touched on. Rather, the focus of the reference is the careless crowd who went heedlessly about their routines and pleasures, drinking and eating and marrying and giving in marriage – all of which presumes a future – while around them the clouds of the Deluge gathered.

So the context of the parable in Matthew is catastrophe whose imminence is undiscerned. In Luke the context is, as we have noted, the story of 'The Doorkeeper', and its effect therefore is one of contrast. The link is made between the two gospel versions in identical comments rounding off each version of the parable: 'Therefore you also must be ready, for the Son of Man is coming at an unexpected hour.'

What to Noah would be in the end a means of blessing, and a fresh beginning, and a rainbow covenant with God, was to his peers catastrophic. What to the doorkeeper and his fellow servants was a blessing, *could* have been, had they fallen short of readiness, a catastrophe. The coming of the Son of Man can be experienced as horror or joy: it depends on 'right humanness'. So now we are ready to look in a little more detail at the parable.

The story
The wording of the parable is very similar in the two gospels, introduced by a strong attention-catching phrase, 'Know this!': rather like the captain's voice over the tannoy of a ship, alerting all personnel with the phrase, 'Now hear this, now hear this'. For where the 'Doorkeeper' parable was for reassurance, *this* parable is for warning. They are the obverse and reverse of the same truth: the necessity of 'knowing the times', of being so 'rightly human' in relation to God that 'readiness' has become one's state of being.

The thumbnail sketch is vivid and recognisable. Security mea-

sures against burglars do not really change through either time
or culture. They involve, in particular, covering the hours of
darkness, a detail noted by Matthew: 'If the owner of the house
had known *in what part of the night* the thief was coming . . .'.
Using 'night' as the point of vulnerability leads naturally into
the insistence that the householder 'would have stayed awake'.
Staying awake and therefore alert is a constant image in Christ's
teaching of that state of the human spirit precisely opposed to
the lassitude and vulnerability of drowsiness. One is reminded
of Gethsemane, and the significant action there of Jesus struggling with horror while his disciples are 'sleeping, for their eyes
were heavy' ('sleeping for sorrow' as Luke puts it).

So, by association, we are taken in Matthew's version of the
parable into the metaphoric mode at this point. Being spiritually
drowsy means being unprepared when the moment of spiritual
crisis comes.

But here the 'similitude' gives us difficulties. For that for
which we must be alert is, in both versions, the 'coming of the
Son of Man' – according to the final comment appended to
the story. But the Christ is no burglar: so how are we to read
this?

The *obvious* point of the parable is that burglars break into
houses where watch is not kept, and steal what is precious.
That is a reality which addresses us all, through time and varied
culture. *Therefore* it behoves us to be watchful at all times, as
the best defence against thieving is of 'being prepared'. Thus
far metonymically. How does the metaphor cut across this?
Two details, one explicit, one implied, may help us. First, that
the house is 'broken into': it is the language of violence. And,
second, that the object of such action must be the taking away
from its true owner of something precious.

May it not be, therefore, that *for us* the metaphoric mode of
the story addresses the truth of the soul's ultimate encounter
with God, as expressed in the final 'coming' of the Son of Man?
We are the householders, each living in the house of the soul.
That ultimate encounter is always, in apocalyptic language,
attended by crisis: by 'violence', in history (possibly simply our
personal history) and in the spiritual world. And we can, at
that moment, if we are not on the alert, if we are unprepared,
lose the thing most precious of all: our *selves*.

For Christ's first listeners the meaning of the story would in metonymic terms refer not only to everyday thievery, but to the constant political dangers, in an occupied country, of the looting attending political unrest and civil disorder. And behind that, for them, would be the metaphoric meaning of the Coming of the One Awaited, the Messiah, who would most surely come – *had* come? – and for whom they must be alert. For the religious leaders that metaphoric mode could have the additional sting: 'Are you alert enough? Has not someone, perhaps, "stolen" your most precious truth, and, taking it away from you, given it elsewhere?' For the early Church it would mean 'Stay alert, for the Lord shall surely return: do not let, through lack of alertness, that precious truth you hold be stolen and lost.'

But for us, reading it as we approach the second millennium, it is a challenge both corporately and personally. Personally: how prepared are we, in this secular and cynical age, for the housebreakers of the soul? And corporately, as the Church: how alert are we to the silent violence of those who break in and privily steal that most precious truth we are charged to guard? Stay awake! for the Son of Man will require that charge at our hands . . .

'Going Before the Judge' (Matt. 5:25, 26; Luke 12:58)

'Preparedness' can mean not simply being 'alert', but being 'knowledgeable' (as any examination candidate will tell us). It is *this* aspect of 'readiness' which Luke's version of this story is emphasising: the kind of 'knowledge' which comes from experience and constant practice, creating a capacity to 'read the times', to make a wise judgement about the meaning of certain signs.

For Luke embeds this parable in material consonant with the 'little apocalypse' of Matthew and Mark we noted earlier, where Jesus speaks of the imminence of 'Judgement' and castigates his listeners because they so knowledgeably read the signs of the weather but cannot read the signs of the (spiritual) times. Yet these latter are of far more ultimate importance to their well-being and, indeed, ultimate survival. 'You know how to interpret the appearance of earth and sky' [the cloud rising in the west, the south wind blowing], 'but why do you not know how to interpret the present time?' (Luke 12:54–56). This ignorance, this lack of discrimination concerning the nature of the present time shows itself, Jesus presses, in their need to go to the law court to resolve disputes: 'Why do you not judge for yourselves what is right?' And thus is introduced the parable of 'Going Before the Judge'.

Matthew's context for the parable is, superficially, quite different. He embeds it in the Sermon on the Mount, where Jesus is urging not simply the adoption of a code of conduct, as in the Law, but the interiorising of this so that it becomes an attitude of the heart. The moment at which this is most tested is at the point of worship. For if the worshipper has behaved towards his fellows with anger or contempt in his heart, then he is in no condition to make a true offering to God. Therefore he must first go and be reconciled, and then return and make his offering. And at this point Matthew recounts Jesus' parable, before continuing in the same vein, that just as there must not only be no murder, but also no anger, so there must not only be no adultery, but no self-indulgence in lustful thoughts: by so doing 'you have already committed adultery . . . in your heart'.

The common context

But while Matthew's emphasis is on a continued way of living, and Luke's is on recognising the imminence of The End, the difference is not as great as it seems. For behind both is a concept of Judgement. In Matthew's account Jesus is arguing that if human law truly mirrored God's – as Jewish Law proposed – then the attitude of the heart would be as critical as any actual actions, and one would be open to the judgement of the Law not only for murder, rape and adultery but for the cast of mind out of which they ultimately grow. Behind any discussion of the Law's judgement lies in such a passage the notion of divine Judgement: and indeed there is reference to being 'liable to the hell of fire' on account of a contemptuous attitude to one's fellows.

This reference to 'fire' takes us back to Luke's context. For it begins from Jesus' reference to himself as coming 'to bring fire to the earth, and how I wish it were already kindled' (12:49). The reference is not only to the Judgement of God which his very presence is ushering in, but – for his listeners – to that moment of judgement in their national history, when the figure of Elijah confronted the prophets of Baal and called down fire from heaven. So this parable is told in the double context of an analogy with a famous prophetic confrontation with misleading religious leaders, as well as of Jesus' (astonishing) claim to be bringing the fire of the divine Judgement. The 'baptism' he refers to (12:49) is a traditional image of 'ordeal': and the 'division' even amidst households which he will bring – outrageous to Jewish ethic – is itself a sign of the 'disturbance' of the Last Times. Taken together, these are the 'signs' his listeners should 'read' as portents of God's decisive action on earth.

So we may take as common context to the parable the reality of God's (imminent) Judgement, the disturbances which attend it, and the need for not just right actions but a right attitude of heart, to be able to judge the evil and the good and recognise the signs of God. Neither the law courts (Luke) nor the Temple Courts (Matthew) are adequate for this: only the interiorising of the Law of God so that knowing his times will be as natural as recognising the signs of coming rain or scorching heat.

The story
And so to the story. It is a little vignette of stern law pursuing its inexorable way. We have to remember that for Jesus' listeners it would express the utmost rigour, since Jewish law did not imprison for debt and this would therefore be – if it were a case of debt – the imposition of secular law. In fact, though this is usually read as a 'debt' case, the charges are not made specific, and it is only the reference at the end of the tale to 'paying every last penny' which suggests that 'debt' is at the heart of the story. 'Paying the last penny' might perhaps equally mean meeting a heavy fine, or distraint of goods.

In fact the nature of the accusation is not important. Rather, it is the process of inexorable law which catches our imagination. Jesus may in fact have been referring to a particular local case. Whether or not, being caught up inescapably in the process would be something familiar to his countrymen, living as they did under both Jewish and Roman law. Its steady grinding on is caught clearly in the metonymic detail, accuser handing the defendant over to the magistrate, and thus to the judge, and so to the officer/guard and finally to prison. From which there is no escape till the last 'penny' is paid – the actual term means one quarter of an 'as', the smallest coin in Roman currency, one hundredth of a denarius.

So much for the realistic, metonymic mode of the parable. As we have seen, its language takes us naturally into the divine Law *behind* the human one: and terms such as 'accuser' and 'judge' have their potency in the religious arena as in the secular one. How then are we to read the metaphor? The contexts have given us the clue. In Matthew's context there is an insistence on being reconciled with one's brother before returning to the altar to make ritual atonement. In other words, religious ritual alone cannot set one right. First one must be reconciled – in other words, *return one's brother to life.* 'Anger' is the equivalent of 'murder', so one has, in one's heart, killed one's brother. Reconciliation returns him to life: only then is the Temple ritual of atonement appropriate and effective in the divine accept-ance of penitence, and absolution of the sin comitted. We may understand therefore in the phrase 'coming to terms with one's accuser' in the parable, that the 'accuser' is both one's brother and *The* Accuser, that unholy angel who denounces one before God's great Tribunal (cf. Rev. 12:10; Job 1:9–11). We are caught up in the inexorable processes, that is, of divine Judgement. The warning is to be reconciled *before* that Great Tribunal takes place. For, once caught up in it, the cost will be totally destructive.

Luke's context brings us to the same metaphoric meaning. For he relates their not being 'able to judge for themselves what is right' to being caught up in the process of law, but this time of divine Law. Prepare yourselves to know right from wrong: as in Matthew's context, make the Law part of your very soul. For otherwise you will be caught up in the Great Tribunal which is God's Judgement; how can you possibly meet what penalty that will impose upon you?

For his first listeners Jesus' meaning is clear. They were a people who had not taken seriously the power of the Accuser, who had not so written the Law of God on their hearts that they were able to know the times, judge both good and evil, and set right their lives before being swept up in the divine Trial. They were in the position of unwitting defendants, not taking seriously the imminence of the Law Court and the pun-ishment which would follow it.

And what for us is the impact of this parable? Not least, to recognise that the attitude of our hearts is as open to judgement as any *actions* we take. And that judgement is already taking place, since we live in the presence of the living Christ. Divine judgement is real, and in Christ it is present: what is seriously amiss is our deferring coming to terms with it, our heedlessness of its immediacy, and our frightening ignorance which leaves us unprepared to recognise the nature of our world's crisis and respond alertly.

But there is of course more. For we live on this side of the Crucifixion and the Resurrection. And therefore that right fear, that we cannot pay the debt even with our last penny, is met by a right thankfulness, that the debt has in fact been paid for us, and that against our Accuser stands a powerful Advocate on our behalf. Because of that, and only that, the parable need not strike us down with fear, though Christ's urging that those listening should 'settle the case' before being caught up in the harsh processes of law does not lose its urgency. Rather it presses upon us the need to 'come to terms' with *him*, and who he is. And that quickly, for who knows? For this listener or that reader, that Great Tribunal might even be tonight.

'The Children in the Marketplace' (Matt. 11:16–19; Luke 7:31–35)

We may regard this micro-parable as a little coda to those we have just looked at: Jesus tells it in the context of speaking to the crowds about John the Baptist, after the latter's inquiry from prison seeking confirmation of Christ's Messiahship. In Matthew's account it is followed by Jesus' denunciation of those Jewish cities where he has preached and not been heard, words of life which places like Tyre and Sidon – those symbols of Gentile profligacy – would have seized gladly, and turned about their way of life, and repented.

Jesus uses this reference to John the Baptist, therefore, to underline that no religious message pleases or satisfies these listeners, both the crowds around him and their religious leaders. For John brought a stern summons to repentance, living with great austerity, and the power of his message was discounted because his hearers, unable to conceive of such discipline, decided he was 'possessed' ('he has a demon'). By contrast, Jesus came amongst them preaching the glorious news of the Kingdom of God, and sharing with them in their wine and food; so they discounted the power of *his* message too, calling him 'a glutton and a drunkard' who had as his friends the outsiders, outlawed by their offence against religious law. The accusation of gluttony and drunkenness puts him in default of the Law (Deut. 21:20) and so deserving of condemnation.

As a result, the word of God is lost to these people. And this is the context of the little story.

The story

The children in the marketplace are playing at weddings and funerals, one group creating the music and the other performing the actions. They play the music of the 'round dance', the men's dance at a wedding: but the boys don't want to dance it. So they sing the mourning song of a funeral (normally sung by women), but the girls will not join in. Nothing pleased! So the business of weddings and funerals might not go ahead, those rituals of the significant moments of life itself.

This is a piece of pure metonymic detail, and we catch vividly the marketplace scene, with the quarrelling and noise from the children. They are, of course – and not just in their imitation of weddings and funerals – mimicking their elders. For those same adults they mimic are *also* immature, also rejecting of all the possibilities, joyful and stern, being offered to them. And so nothing creative can happen that day, either in the lives of the children or – metaphorically – in the lives of the adults they reflect.

We can go further. The four parables we have looked at reflect both the grace and the sternness of God's Law; they reflect both divine mercy and divine justice. But there is the terrible danger that Jesus' hearers in his own day will be prepared to accept neither, the one because it is too 'lenient', the other because it is too 'harsh'. And the same danger attends us today. We are unwilling to respond to the tune God plays; when its emphasis is on the absoluteness of his justice we repudiate it as over-exacting and unacceptable. When its emphasis is on the – equal – absoluteness of his grace, we try to hedge it round with provisos and rules: it is too magnanimous for our liking.

So we do not join in the divine Game, and instead sit carping on the side. Not recognising that this Game is the name of reality, the only reality there is: and that if we are not alert to it, ready to take part in it, and so fail to join the Game, it will pass us by and others will be drawn into it. And leave us, at the end, with no Game to play.

9 The Parables of 'The Temporary Manager', 'The Ten Bridesmaids', 'The Guest Without a Wedding Garment' and 'The Rich Fool'

THE FOUR PARABLES we are to read in this chapter continue the theme which links those of the last: that of 'preparedness'. In Hamlet's words 'the readiness is all'. There is an extra dimension to these four (which can also be found in some other parables), which it is worth looking at briefly, before we examine them individually. For behind the issue of 'readiness' in each of these is a further one: that of responsibility, accountability; and that accountability is for something to which one can claim no *right* of oneself. That which is 'loaned' to the managerial servant of the first story is 'authority'. The bridesmaids and the guest at the wedding feast have been offered 'participation'. The rich and unwise man has been 'loaned' his very life. None of them has come to terms with the truth of his or her status, so each is unprepared. In other words, what we have in these stories is a hint at some of the attitudes or motives or factors *because of* which human beings are unprepared for the great and decisive moment of their lives, the moment when they must meet the just and merciful reality of God.

'The Temporary Manager' (Matt. 24:45–51; Luke 12:42–46)

This little parable appears in much the same context in both gospel accounts, following the 'Burglar' parable, with its concluding comment: 'You also must be ready for the Son of Man coming at an unexpected hour.' However, there are some significant differences between the two contexts and versions. For in Matthew the story proper is immediately followed by the parable of 'The Ten Bridesmaids', whereas in Luke's account there is an addition – a scale of punishment – added at the end of the parable which clearly relates to what immediately precedes the story here. For after the 'Burglar' story Luke describes Peter as asking whether that parable was 'for us or for everyone?' (12:41). Jesus' oblique reply is this story of the servant given temporary managerial authority. Luke's account – after describing the different levels of punishment awaiting those 'managers' who knew, or did not know, their master's wishes, and failed to honour them – goes on to Jesus' references to the 'fire' he was to bring, the 'baptism' he was to endure, and the parable of 'Going Before the Judge'.

From this it will be clear that the emphasis of the story was discerned slightly differently by the two gospel writers, and both of them had rather altered that emphasis from the natural thrust of the parable – as we shall see. For Matthew the story has become, by its end, explicitly a story about the suddenness, the unexpectedness, of the Last Day, which for the early Church would also be the Day of Christ's Coming. The phrase 'weeping and gnashing of teeth' firmly places the climax of the story in a beyond-this-world place of punishment. The phrase is the traditional one to describe the horror of despair of those condemned, because of what they recognise as their own folly, to 'outer darkness.' Put with the earlier comment that the returned master, discovering that his temporary manager has disgracefully neglected his duties, 'will cut him off' (not 'in pieces' – probably a misreading) and 'put him with the hypocrites', it is clear that the story has become one of *eternal* rewards and punishments. Presumably the early Church would read it as an admonition to faithfulness while the Lord's Second Coming was delayed. It is, therefore, yet another example of the way the parables were read by the young Christian community in a way which assisted in the enormous shift of faith-perception and understanding which had to take place, as the period before the Second Coming, at first understood as imminent, was slowly recognised as a wait for an indefinite period, but a wait which would end most suddenly, without warning, exposing the reality or otherwise of the faith of each follower of Christ. Matthew's account and 'placing' of the story, therefore, is admonitory, urging *faithfulness* on all the followers of Christ, however long the delay.

The fact that Luke recounts the story as an answer to Peter's question gives this demand for faithfulness a slightly different edge in his account. For the implication is that the parable applies to the disciples themselves; indeed this might well be understood as *specifically* the Twelve, the Apostles. They have been entrusted, on Jesus' departure, with temporary authority on his behalf: as indeed the Seventy had been during his lifetime (Luke 10:1). This authority was to give the household 'the allowance of food at the proper time', in other words to look after its commissariat. It is easy to see how the early Church would interpret this as a charge to the Church's leaders, to care for it till their Lord came. The sanctions added at the end indicate how, even if those in charge were not clear about what were their master's wishes, they would be understood to be 'responsible' though less blameworthy than he who *did* know 'what his master wanted' and ignored it; who would 'receive a severe beating'. One is reminded of Paul's reference to Christian leaders who fail in their responsibilities:

> *The work of each builder will become visible, for the Day will disclose it, because it will be revealed with fire, and fire will test what sort of work each has done. If what has been built on the foundation survives, the builder will receive a reward. If the work is burned up, the builder will suffer loss; the builder will be saved, but only as through fire.* (1 Cor. 3:13–15)

So much for the gospel writers' understanding of the parable. How would Jesus' first listeners hear it? Clearly its main point is less that of suddenness than of how far those trusted with temporary responsibility for 'the household' have honoured that trust. The 'household of God' would surely be understood as their nation Israel: and that God was implied in the parable was clear from the reference to 'the master' consigning the failed servant to the place of 'the hypocrites' (Matthew), 'the unfaithful' (Luke), where there would be 'weeping and gnashing of teeth'. Those with 'delegated authority' in Israel would inevitably be seen as its religious leaders; and the sudden return of the master 'on a day when he did not expect him, and at an hour he did not know' would be understood as referring to the Last Day.

A reading of the story for today
But standing in the aftermath of the Incarnation, Crucifixion and Resurrection, we can see this story as told by the 'house-

hold's' master himself. There is a double focus here, in that, even as he tells the story, he has indeed come and discovered that the servants with temporary authority have abused its power over his household, though some are faithfully 'at work'. The religious leadership of Israel has not met what was asked of it. Yet that religious leadership has not, even now, recognised that its master is suddenly come. So the story is as yet not fully worked out.

But how can we read this parable as addressing ourselves, today? Its metonymy is simple and clear. A large estate, familiar throughout that countryside. An owner away for a long period, appointing from among his household of slaves a temporary agent or manager to be in charge of the slaves, explicitly 'to give them their allowance of food at the proper times'. In other words, to ensure the commissariat, and the leisure to enjoy it, was properly ordered. From this situation the parable develops, still within the metonymy of this familiar world, two alternative, equally familiar endings. *Either*, the master comes home suddenly and finds 'that slave at work when he arrives'. In such case the slave is 'blessed', and the master will promote him from the simple care of the household's commissariat to being 'in charge of all his possessions'. *Or* the master comes home to find this temporary manager has told himself that his master is 'delayed', i.e., he no longer believes in his return – and so he begins 'to beat the other men and women', and to 'eat and drink and get drunk'.

How does the metaphoric mode cut across this? The additions by the two gospel writers put aside, the story ends with the fate of the irresponsible servant, 'apportioned with the unbelieving' (or 'with the hypocrites'). Such language takes us beyond the familiar world of household management, to a household bonded by 'belief' or 'integrity'. So that we now look again at what 'authority' is being temporarily invested in this agent. It is that of ensuring the *continued nourishment* of a household with a 'common calling', a common ethos.

'Authority' is vested by the master in the servant for the supervision and nourishment of his people. It is difficult to avoid reading this first, in our day, as effectively addressing those formally given delegated authority over Christ's household: the ordained, or the formally appointed leaders of the Church. How does the parable speak to such? If they are found 'at work' when the master comes, then they are 'blessed' – their state is one of joy – and greater responsibility will be theirs: they will indeed share with their Lord care for 'all his possessions'. But what may we understand, in the metaphoric mode, by such a one 'beating' his or her fellows, 'eating and drinking with drunkards'? Is not the point of such description a loss of the sense that the 'authority' was but *loaned*, and is not a personal possession? It is being abused: the temporary manager's fellows are being bullied and his powers used to indulge his own priorities and pleasures. Moreover, in our wider understanding, God's household extends beyond the Church to the world, since all humanity shares a common calling. How well has the responsibility for feeding it spiritually been maintained? Does the Church 'beat' or 'nourish' the world?

And further: at the heart of this parable there is the indictment which addresses every age, including our own: that *humanity* has been given 'temporary management', spiritually and physically, in the earth. Where this has been recognised as stewardship of the Master's household – the world in which we live – and faithfully undertaken as accountable to him, 'blessing' will follow, and, the promise runs, an ever greater share in the care of all God's domain. But where we arrogantly abrogate such authority to ourselves and use violence on that we should be stewarding, pursuing heedlessly our own self-indulgences – there we shall find ourselves confronted by the true Authority, stripped of our pretensions, and excluded from the domain we have abused.

And so we reach the centre of the parable. It is the Genesis story all over again: the usurpation of an authority and mandate temporary and loaned by God for his own purposes of blessing. As a human society, as a Christian community, as leaders of the Church, we may be 'unready', 'unprepared' for the unexpected sudden appearance of the God who calls us to account. But on the other hand – for this is a tale of equal blessing and cursing – we may indeed be 'ready', 'prepared', found at work in our 'household'.

That sudden 'appearing' has already happened in human history, and in Christ's continued presence with us is inherent in every moment of our lives. But its ultimate will be in the consummation of human history to which the Christian faith points forward. This little parable is one of the signposts on that way.

'The Ten Bridesmaids' (Matt. 25:1–13) and 'The Guest Without a Wedding Garment' (Matt. 22:11–14)

These two well-known parables have more in common than that they both centre on a wedding! For both are concerned with 'readiness', and in both the possibility of 'participation' which has been offered is not one by 'right'; so, within both, that participation is forfeited because of failure to 'prepare'. Thus much for the basic 'plot' of each parable.

The context
Both these parables appear only in Matthew's gospel. The 'Bridesmaids' story follows the parables of 'The Burglar' and 'The Temporary Manager', and is itself followed by 'The Talents'; so that it is clearly interconnected in the mind of the writer of the gospel with the themes of these three. The story of 'The Guest Without a Wedding Garment' is appended to a longer parable, that of 'The Great Banquet', whose main point (as we shall see) it actually seems at odds with. Matthew has thus positioned it in the series of parables set immediately after the entry into Jerusalem, where Jesus' confrontation with the religious authorities is open, explicit, and very sharp – so much so that Matthew comments, 'When the chief priests and the Pharisees heard his parables, they realized that he was speaking about them. They wanted to arrest him' (Matt. 21:45, 46a).

'The Ten Bridesmaids'

Matthew concludes this story with the admonition, 'Keep awake therefore, for you know neither the day nor the hour' (Matt. 25:13). He therefore clearly understands its emphasis to be on the suddenness, the unexpectedness, of the bridegroom's appearance, so that the failure of the 'foolish' bridesmaids is, like that of the temporary manager and the owner of the burgled house, that they have been 'caught napping'. So for him, in the context of the early Church, the story was one of the sequence of parables about Christ's delayed Second Coming, and the need for his followers to remain faithfully and alertly prepared. Phrases such as 'as the bridegroom was delayed', 'but at midnight there was a shout, "Look! Here is the bridegroom"', are crucial to this. Christ in such a reading is the heavenly Bridegroom and the wedding feast is the Great Feast of his triumph in heaven in the End-Time. The parable would most helpfully, its emphasis thus re-understood, speak to the condition of the young and expectant Christian community.

The original focus of the story is clearly rather different. For one thing all ten of the bridesmaids slept, the wise as well as the foolish, so 'sleeping' was clearly not the point at issue. The specific difference between the two groups is explicitly that 'when the foolish took their lamps, they took no oil with them; but the wise took flasks of oil with their lamps'. So lack of preparation *in order to sustain* their attendance on the bridegroom was their fault. Hence they have to leave their place of watching in order to repair their omission; and in their absence the looked-for one comes, they miss him, and they are shut out from the celebrations.

How would the crowd, and among them the religious leaders, 'hear' this? The Messiah as 'bridegroom' is a late image not found prior to Christian writing: so they would not naturally see this story as to do with the 'Coming One'. The two sharp features of the story are the unpreparedness of some of those waiting, when at last without warning the looked-for Event happens; and the exclusion from the Feast. It is likely, therefore, that the story would have been heard as one of warning, that some of those looking to *usher in* the Event of Celebration were ill-prepared, and could find themselves excluded. Since the 'bridesmaids' are part of the official retinue of the ceremony and the celebration, this would at one level imply to the crowd that their status as a nation 'ushering in' the celebrations of God should not be taken for granted: not all of them would find themselves prepared. More precisely, it would obviously apply to their religious leaders.

'The Guest Without a Wedding Garment'

Properly this story starts in Matt. 22:2 and then leaps over
verses 3–10, starting again at verse 11. For it has been yoked
with Matthew's account of 'The Great Banquet' (a story Luke
also tells (14:16–24), but with different details and without the
addition of 'The Guest without a Wedding Garment'). We shall
be reading this parable later (in Chapter 13) but we need to
note here that its main thrust, though expressed even more
strongly in Luke than in Matthew, is the filling of the banqueting hall from the crowds in the streets, an unlikely and
(one would have thought) ill-prepared gathering of guests. The
story of 'The Guest Without a Wedding Garment' is locked on
to this not only by sequence, but by its concluding comment
'For many are called but few are chosen' (22:14).

So clearly Matthew has 'placed' it there as a corrective. The
'Great Banquet' has been opened up to everyone 'both good
and bad', so that the hall was filled. For the early Christian
community this could clearly be dangerously misinterpreted as
freeing all who would come of any kind of moral responsibility.
(We have noted before this was an anxiety Paul also addressed.)
Hence the addition of this parable at this point, which instantly
alters – particularly by its concluding comment – the 'free for
all' of the 'Great Banquet' story. The thrust of this parable insists
that *though* the invitation is to everyone, 'good and bad', yet
not all will be allowed to stay. As Bunyan put it, there is a way
to hell even from the gate of heaven itself. The distinction is
made, therefore, between the *invitation* to grace, which in the
teeth of his nation's religious opposition Christ radically opened
up and which the gospel writers faithfully record; and *assimi-
lation* into the Christian community. Presumably the young
Church, in its missionary expansion, discovered the need to
affirm some necessary conditions of membership, and found in
this parable of the 'wedding garment' a helpful model. What
that Christian community might have understood by the necessary 'garment' we can now only guess. Repentance? Faith?
Either of these seems possible. In both cases the point is that
the guest has not 'fitted himself' for the gathering and the
occasion – the great celebration of the Feast in heaven of
the King's Son, the Bridegroom. He has been heedless of the
need for *preparing* for such an occasion.

If we set aside what is implied by its positioning, and look to the story 'free-standing', so to speak, how might the original listeners have heard it? That God's coming Kingdom was like a wedding feast, to which one must come with proper preparation as one did in one's own community. Without it, one could lose one's place at table, and be ushered out, into a darkness thicker by contrast with the brightness within. At the Last Day, the chief cause of despair ('weeping and gnashing of teeth') would be that one had been given the opportunity and failed to take it, through casualness in preparation. For the crowd this could sound like the challenge to ready themselves to respond properly to the invitation which nationally, as the people of God, they had received. To the religious leaders, almost certainly, it would seem a direct attack on themselves – already seated, as it were, at the King's table, and turned out at the last moment because they were not fitted to be there.

A current reading of the stories:
(i) 'The Ten Bridesmaids'
First, the metonymic detail giving us a coherent picture. It is quite possible Jesus is using an actual local wedding and incidents connected with it, which his hearers would recognise. Marriage customs vary so much even locally, and from century to century, that some of the detail we have here we have to accept as realistic without knowing the full facts. Certainly throughout this part of the world the procession of the bridegroom, either to the bride's house or returning with her to his own, was formal and highly ceremonial. Since the wedding feast of the story began when the bridegroom came it is clear that at this point bride and groom were together. Since they were the *bride's* maids coming out to meet the bridegroom, it looks as though the picture emerging is of their forming a kind of 'guard of honour' as he arrives at the bride's home.

There has been a good deal of discussion about their oil lamps, what shape they were and why they needed oil: the ordinary 'slipper'-shaped lamp seems inappropriate, and it is possible ceremonial torches were what is implied, their head wrapped in oil-soaked rags. It is not important, since this is not an allegory. What is vital is to catch the vignette as a realistic snapshot of a traditional wedding festivity of people of some substance, complete with processions and wedding feast. (And of nearby shops staying open all night selling – among other things – oil for lamps!)

The metaphoric mode begins with the characterisation of the ten bridesmaids as soon as they are introduced, as 'five foolish, five wise'. Since 'wisdom' is an aspect of godliness in Jewish thinking, and 'folly' as behaving as though there were no God, the story is instantly opening out into a religious dimension. The more so because externally there is nothing to distinguish the one group from the other. They all carry lamps, they all grow drowsy, they all sleep. The only objective sign of distinction is that five have *thought ahead* and been prepared for such eventualities as delay; and five have not. Five, therefore, have been much more alert to reality, the way things really are, than their counterparts. The improvident ones are forced to rush away, as in a bad dream, to make good their lack. But it is pointless, for when they come panting back they are too late. Too late for what? For *doing the task* for which they had been included in the first place, that of 'going out to meet the bridegroom', and light him on his way. So of course when they knock at the door, he does not know them; they had not fulfilled their calling, they were not part of the welcome party who greeted him and thereby made themselves known to him, by being participants with him. So they are excluded.

How can this, metaphorically, address us today? One of the key elements in the story seems to be that all that distinguished those 'included' from those 'excluded' was something not at first glance visible; an attitude of mind, an inherent folly which did not take seriously the task in hand and what lay ahead. In religious terms, this story assumes as fact the critical event, the encounter with the 'bridegroom', the founder of the feast; that is, with God himself. If we are called to any task which will help 'celebrate' him, then this is a serious matter we must attend to thoughtfully. The community of believers today, as in the past, is in such a position. And like the bridesmaids, it is not at all easy to tell among this community who is properly preparing to celebrate God, and who is not. So there is a danger the Christian communiy might assume that it does not matter, and no distinction will be made.

But, if I read this parable aright as it addresses us in *our* century (as in past centuries), there is grave warning here. Having in other parables been reminded by Jesus that others' exclusion is a matter for sorrow, not joy, we are now warned that nevertheless some people *will exclude themselves*, and those people *may be us*. For if we have taken no steps to ensure we are ready and prepared for our encounter with God, whenever that might come, to do our task of living for him ('carrying our lamps') and to be known of him, then we are 'outside' the ambience of joy and celebration which others, who have cared more, share with him. We are unfitted by our whole way of being to be there with them. And so, not only are we excluded from what is going on: we are separated out *by virtue of what we have let ourselves become*, appearances having been overtaken by reality.

It is a frightening parable, none the less so for being so familiar that it has almost been tamed. Almost. The concepts of *separation* from those with whom we had apparently shared a calling, and *exclusion* from the ultimate life together, as a result of our own heedlessness, uncaring and laziness, is not one that lodges easily in our current culture. Yet the parable probes us. In the end, it says, is not this the truth of how things ultimately work? Then why should it not be so in your encounter with God?

A current reading:
(ii) *'The Guest Without a Wedding Garment'*

'Wedding garments' were not necessarily new, but freshly washed, smartened up in honour of the occasion. To appear with a grubby robe was to be insulting to the host, an essential metonymic detail in this little parable; as is the fact that as a matter of courtesy in this culture the host did not eat with his guests, but made an appearance during the meal so that he could move round among them for conversation.

So what we have at the metonymic level is one of the great parties at which many guests are present, and among whom the host is moving – in this story it is a king at the wedding banquet for his son. The feast could be well on its way, therefore, before this particular guest is discovered.

The second metonymic stage of the story occurs when the king accosts him, asking by what right he is there ('How did you get in here?'). It is courteously done; 'Friend', he says, thereby implying (a) that he does not know him and (b) that there is cause for reproach. (On the three occasions this form of address is used in the New Testament (Matt. 20:13; 22:12; 26:50), the person addressed is in the wrong: i.e. the parable of 'The Good Employer', this parable, and Christ's word to Judas in Gethsemane at the moment of betrayal.) Yet at this stage the situation could still be retrievable, if the guest had responded with either sound reason, or apology. But – the most curious detail – 'he was speechless' (literally 'he was silenced'). He had nothing to say for himself. 'Struck dumb' would catch the mood; or 'his tongue stuck to the roof of his mouth'.

This is still just within the metonymic bounds, since gate-crashing a party and being discovered and publicly questioned could well, realistically, leave one with nothing to say. So, too, the host's adjuration to the attendants to 'throw him out'. But binding him hand and foot, and consigning him to outer dark-ness, is clearly the language of metaphor. So metaphor and metonymy become interwoven at this point. In what other ways does the metaphoric mode work?

There are two other obvious points where the metaphor is engaged. The first is concerning the nature of the 'robe' or 'garment' the guest should be wearing to fit himself for this place and moment. The second is this crucial detail of 'speech-lessness'. What do they add to the meaning of the story?

The image of being 'clothed' in order to be fit for the ultimate moment is an archetypal one. Jesus referred to Isaiah 61 a number of times, and v. 10 in that chapter runs:

> For he has clothed me with the garments of salvation,
>   he has covered me with the robe of righteousness.

It is worth remembering that in our reading of 'The Prodigal Son and the Loving Father' we noted the importance of the father 'putting upon' his returned son 'the best robe' (i.e. the ceremonial one) so that he had transformed him into the sonship that was being offered back to him. And the image is strongly present, of course, in the book of Revelation. The concept is older and more widespread even than biblical examples, and anthropologists could no doubt help us on its range and richness. But there is no doubt the Bible focuses through it the notion of moral and spiritual transformation being expressed *through* the offered garment *by* the generosity of someone else: most probably, the host. Hence New Testament images of redemption and salvation as 'robes', 'new clean clothes' (compare Luke 8:35: 'They found the man from whom the demons had gone, sitting at the feet of Jesus, clothed and in his right mind').

So we may understand the lack of appropriate garment here as indicating this guest has not accepted (not seen the need for?) any such transforming 'robe'. He therefore is at odds with his surroundings and those amongst whom he sits. Now, if we think of banquets and wedding feasts and indeed parties generally, what characterises them is first that people have gone to the trouble of making themselves look festive, fresh and clean, in honour of the host and the occasion. And second, that they *talk* to each other. Such an occasion is for communication, for chatter, for engaging with each other in enjoyment and purely for the sake of enjoyment.

But this man was 'speechless'. He therefore did not fit on the second count either. His dress gave no signal that he understood the nature of the occasion, and he was unable to enter into the primary activity (other than eating) of the occasion. It does not mean he was afflicted with dumbness. It means he could find nothing to say. He did not know the language of the feast.

And so, like the foolish bridesmaids, he is excluded, separated out from the rest of the party, and set outside in the darkness, in despair at having by his own folly come to this point. Again, it is a difficult parable for our own culture to take to itself. It suggests that in the wonders of the celebration which, faith declares, lies ahead for all those who love God (which the earlier parable had suggested was a far more diverse group than the rigorists had believed), there will be those who are self-excluded, because they have not thought it necessary to learn the language of heaven and seek the transforming garment of active grace, *forgiveness* (both receiving it and themselves offering it to others) which would fit them for what was to come. Like the parable of the bridesmaids, it is not a parable to apply to any other person. It is a parable to apply to oneself.

'The Rich Fool' (Luke 12:16–25)

Luke places this famous parable as a commentary by Jesus on
a judgement he has been asked, and refused, to give. As he is
teaching the crowds, a man among them, clearly much seized
in his mind by his own grievances, recognises in Jesus the
quality of 'authority', and begs him to sort out the family row:
'Teacher, tell my brother to divide the family inheritance with
me.' Discerning the rights and wrongs of inheritance law within
the family required specialised training and experience, and
Jesus' 'authority' is of another kind. He disclaims being *that*
kind of 'judge'. What he *is* authoritative about is attitude of
heart: and it is this he immediately probes, arising out of the
situation suggested by the man's request. For at the heart of
the family quarrel it is likely there will be greed, and this he
warns against explicitly: 'Be on your guard against all kinds of
greed' (12:15) 'for one's life does not consist in the abundance
of possessions.' This parable of the 'foolish' rich man then
follows, and after that Luke's version of part of the Sermon on
the Mount, in particular Christ's urging his listeners to 'take no
thought for the morrow', insisting that life was 'more than food'
and the body 'more than clothing'. The 'ravens' and the 'lilies'
were object lessons, could they but read them.

Thus far the context. It means that the parable itself is
addressed to the whole crowd, but in the light of a specific
issue: money, means of living, wealth, and how this related to
quality of living. As such it is both timeless, and free of the
religious controversy out of which so many of Jesus' parables
grew. He was taking a question which was the daily source of
anxiety of virtually everyone who was present, and to most
people who have read the parable since. This is one of the
stories which addresses our own century in terms very little
different from those of his first hearers. So we may begin
immediately to look at its metonymic detail.

The background of the story is of a rich fertile estate, well
managed and producing ever more abundantly. There are barns
on the estate, but they were built before this abundance, and
so they are inadequate. A clear and recognisable picture. And so
is the thinking of the estate's owner. It is the same kind of
thinking as that of a current delighted Lottery winner. Delight,
a certain amount of planning about how to 'invest' – in this

case, store the grain and goods for a long-term future – and then a vision of endless self-indulgence, buttressed by his 'ample goods'. He can 'relax, eat, drink, be merry'.

But that night he dies. 'Where then will be all these things stored up?' Jesus asks. A nice connection here with the 'family inheritance' issue which prompted this story. We have returned, by implication, to the start of the discussion, litigation over the inheritance.

Thus far a complete metonymic picture. But the metaphoric mode is introduced in the rich man's address to himself. 'Soul,' he says, 'you have ample goods.' It is the inner core of the man which is now in the forefront of the story: that which will endure, if anything does. It is this soul which God addresses. And to be called 'fool' is to be warned that one is living as though God did not exist. In this metaphoric mode 'riches towards God' are distinguished from 'treasures for oneself'. The man is found, though abundant in the latter, to be poverty-stricken in the former.

But God's dialogue in the story takes us much further than this. For the words are 'This very night your life is being demanded of you'. That is, the man's life itself is answerable 'on demand', at any time: he holds it only *on loan*. His 'folly' had not been in his delight in the riches, or even in his (sensible) planning, but in the attitude of heart that addressed his soul as *having sufficiency*. Sufficiency, Jesus is saying, is only of God: it is his gift, and he can give or take away as he chooses, yes, very life itself.

So this is not simply a *memento mori*, a warning that death might take us, Christ's latest, as his first, listeners, at any time. It is not a word of kill-joy, of destroying of pleasure. It is a warning against the false self-sufficiency that does not always recognise that life is held on loan from God.

And the context takes us further. For far from being threatening or alarming, Christ is using this parable to probe the motive *behind* this kind of materialism, and replace it with something greater. For the man's address to his soul is about *security* – about having nothing more to fear now for many years to come. The context tells us this, for the whole thrust of what follows in Jesus' teaching on this occasion is summed up in 'Do not be afraid – fear not – little flock,' (so tender a phrase!) 'for it is your Father's good pleasure to give you the kingdom'

(12:32). That is: you are afraid of what life might do to you and so you look to wealth and possessions to give you security. But there is no need to be afraid, for God the Father's plan for you is for good, not evil, in 'the Kingdom', God's domain of grace and fruitfulness. And all round you the natural world is demonstrating that.

So, far from being one of Jesus' minatory parables, though there is warning here, there is also reassurance. To be misled into seeking false kinds of security is to live as though God did not exist: but there is a profounder security, which actually *goes with* the fact that our life is on loan. Trust the One who 'secures' that loan and it will follow that, in the end, that security will not fail. For you will then be ready, prepared, with riches towards God of an indestructible kind.

For us, who read this parable in the context of cosmic uncertainty, on the one hand, and doubt now even about the definition of the point of death, on the other, there is nevertheless an undergirding to this reassurance which Christ's first listeners did not have. For though they stood in the richness of God's very presence in Jesus – and did not know it – we stand in the awed knowledge not only of the fact of that presence then on earth, but of the Resurrection of that life apparently extinguished. So the 'authority' for which that questioner from the crowd looked, those centuries ago, has been affirmed in the only way which could make those reassurances good: by the Teller of the tale himself allowing his life, like that of the rich man, to be demanded of him, and proving, thereafter, the inexhaustible riches of God.

II: COMMITMENT AND OBEDIENCE

10 The Parables of 'The Treasure', 'The Pearl', 'The Tower Builder', 'The King Planning War', 'The Two Houses' and 'The Untrustworthy Manager'

ONCE 'THE TIMES' are discerned, some kind of response to that knowledge must follow. Jesus' parables explore this truth just as his life, his death and his Resurrection enact it. So the group of parables we shall read in this chapter are, with one exception, a series of vignettes on what is required of 'right humanness' once the nature of this revelatory moment has been discerned.

'The Treasure' and 'The Pearl' (Matt. 13:44, 45)

It is when Matthew is recounting in sequence a series of parables which include this pair, that he also comments on Jesus' use of parables as a teaching method.

> Jesus told the crowd all these things in parables; without a parable he told them nothing. This was to fulfil what had been spoken through the prophet:
> 'I will open my mouth to speak in parables;
> I will proclaim what has been hidden from the foundation of the world.' (Matt. 13:34, 35)

We shall be looking much more closely, at the conclusion of this book, at the passage Matthew quotes, but it is worth noting here this ambiguity of Jesus' method. The parables 'proclaim' what has been hidden; or – an equally valid translation – they are 'dark sayings' about things which have always been kept secret. Certainly a distinction is clearly made between the way Jesus taught the crowd, and his commentary afterwards to his disciples. One such commentary, on 'The Wheat and the Weeds', immediately precedes this little pair of parables. The commentary ends with a reference to the Day of Judgement: and, immediately subsequent to this pair of parables, there follows the parable of 'The Dragnet', which also sounds the note of the End-Time. So we have to take seriously that 'The Treasure', and 'The Pearl' refract echoes on the one hand of 'that which has been secret since the foundation of the world', and on the other hand 'that which will be revealed at the end of the world'. And this is our clue, our bridge, into the metaphoric mode of these micro-stories.

For their homely metonymic detail hardly seems to relate to such vast notions. They are nicely balanced, socially. The man who discovers the treasure in the field is poor – perhaps hired labour? – certainly it is not his own field he is working in, and he has to sell all he possesses to buy that one field. The merchant, by contrast, already has a stock to sell. He is likely to be passing through Galilee on his way back from buying pearls at source, where the divers produce them from the Red Sea or the Persian Gulf or even the Indian Ocean. Having amassed his store, he will travel back through Palestine to the great cities where he can sell at considerable profit. But just as he is concluding his negotiations with the divers he comes across a single pearl of such beauty that everything he has acquired heretofore seems paltry.

The labourer in the field hastily re-buries what he has discovered: some container – urn, perhaps, or wine jar – full of coin or jewels. So many wars had been fought across these fields: someone, at sometime, had hastily buried it there for safety, hoping to return when the battle had rolled away. And never did. But burial was still the traditional way of keeping precious things safe, so that is what the finder did. Legally he would not be required to report the find, but the only way he could ensure keeping it unchallenged – make sure it was truly his – was to buy the field. And even though it means selling up everything, it is 'with joy' that he does so.

And so also the merchant, who would have an artist's delight in the fineness of the pearl, as well as the businessman's satisfaction at the potential of what he has found.

So the details in both stories are culturally familiar, integrated, recognisable. But they have another metonymic coherence also. For they are also the stuff of traditional storytelling. The treasure long hidden, now discovered by a poor man; the pearl from the sea bed: where in the wide world will it be sold, and what use will the merchant make of the power it gives him? Both stories would have anticipated endings of a familiar kind: the poor man marrying richly, perhaps, or building a palace or having trains of servants; the merchant perhaps advising kings.

So the unexpected non-development of the story would take Jesus' listeners aback. The point of the story is not, it seems, as it traditionally is, in the treasure or the pearl as a means to an end: the point is in the *discovery*, and *in what the finders did* to make sure of this prize.

So here we begin to enter the metaphoric mode, as the context offers it. The context, reinforced by the phrase, 'the kingdom of heaven is like . . .', emphasises that we are talking about the eternal qualities of the 'kingdom of heaven': that which was true 'from the foundation of the world', through into 'the End-Time' and beyond. And what are the keynotes here? Joy, first of all: the kind of joy which makes everything else unimportant. It is *'the joy of heaven'* we are talking about, the language of divine celebration we have already encountered in other parables. But, second, there is recognition that to obtain the Kingdom of heaven, to make it one's own, is an end in itself, not a means to an end. 'Heaven', a place in God's domain, is all one could ask or want. And, third, therefore everything else is of secondary importance and must, if necessary, be disposed of, in order that one may gain heaven untramelled.

It is worth noticing, too, that there are elements of 'search' ('The Pearl') and 'secrecy' ('The Treasure') in the two stories which accord well with the pattern of the gospels. But the chief insistence is on the one virtue above all: that of total commitment. For it is that which hooks these stories of ordinary life into the language of eternity. Both the treasure-finder and the pearl-seeker have recognised the moment, known the thing for what it was. Beyond that must come *commitment*, or the secret is lost to them. Commitment: 'a condition', as T. S. Eliot wrote, 'of complete simplicity, costing not less than everything'.

'The Tower Builder' and 'The King Planning War' (Luke 14:28–32)

The context in which Luke sets this pair of micro-parables is as Jesus 'turned' to address the 'great crowds' who were 'travelling with him'. But did walking behind or alongside him like this, in a huge mob, in any sense constitute 'following' him? Jesus is at pains to challenge them about any false notions they might have about what they are currently doing.

> 'Whoever comes to me and does not hate father and mother, wife and children, brothers and sisters, yes, and even life itself, cannot be my disciple. Whoever does not carry the cross and follow me cannot be my disciple.' (Luke 14:26)

Matthew has expressed the same teaching in a less stark, more positive way:

> 'Whoever loves father or mother more than me is not worthy of me; and whoever loves son or daughter more than me is not worthy of me; and whoever does not take up the cross and follow me is not worthy of me.' (Matt. 10:37–38)

But in Matthew's account this teaching is a part of Jesus' preparation of the Twelve to go out on his behalf into the countryside and villages. They have already shown their commitment to him to be much greater than rambling after him in curiosity and hope, like the crowds. So while the emphasis is still on total commitment, the style is less harsh in expressing it.

The illustrative pair of stories, however, does not appear in Matthew. In Luke they follow the gruesome challenge about the cross. Some have argued that this must be an editorial addition arising from after-knowledge of the Crucifixion. Indeed, that is plausible; but we must not forget the landscape of Palestine was littered with crosses, the visible reminder of the way Rome punished rebellion in its occupied states. Jesus could have been pointing to one: or to an execution procession. Taken together with the comment rounding off the parables, 'So therefore, none of you can become my disciple if you do not give up all your possessions', it constitutes the most absolute of choices. The issues are not of an exciting jaunt in the wake of an intriguing charismatic wonder-worker to watch and marvel at, but of life and death itself: of choosing a course of action for which one is prepared to pay everything, just as some of the Zealot freedom-fighters did: 'loss of family' (exile?), 'loss of possessions' (punitive distraint of goods?), 'loss of life itself'.

Hence these micro-parables are more powerful (and would be to their first listeners) than on the surface they appear. They express *degrees* of humiliation; it is worth looking closer to see how this works.

In metonymic terms they represent, accurately, two quite different levels of decision-making. In each case the decision is linked with 'enlargement'. The farmer plans to build a tower which will establish him in the eyes of his neighbours as of large and prosperous estate. Again, Jesus could be referring to an actual instance which would have drawn knowing nods and grins from the crowd. But the budget had not been properly balanced and all work had to stop soon after the foundations were laid. There they were, in the grass, a monument to 'folly': to presuming beyond one's capabilities. At the very least the farmer will suffer ridicule where he had looked for admiration or even envy. (He might also suffer worse, since he has over-stretched himself financially.) In the social life of these villages and small towns this is an accurate and coherent picture of how life worked.

And so is the story on the grander scale, that of the king planning war. He must surely 'sit down' (i.e., take time and care) to work out the strategy and its cost: whether his 10,000 troops can possibly withstand the 20,000 coming against him. It is not clear whether in fact he has been the initiator of this offensive, or its victim. That, in the end, is not material. What is at issue is whether his capability is adequate for victory. For if it is not, he would be wise to sue for peace long before battle is joined.

The land where Jesus tells this story was pock-marked with the history of such wars (and still is). So what would be evident to the listeners would be not only the potential disaster for the king, but for the king's people. Loss of family, of goods, of lands, or possessions, of life itself, could follow.

The metaphoric mode of these stories emerges when we compare their immediate apparent meaning with what emerges

on reflection. For Jesus *seems* to be saying that it is better not
to embark on a great endeavour unless one has made quite
sure beforehand that one's resources are adequate for it. In
such cases this would merely be an enlargement of a familiar
proverbial saw such as, in our own culture, 'Look before you
leap'. But the context alone would indicate more than this, as
a further look at the stories reveals. For Jesus is addressing the
crowd: that same crowd, hungry for bread and miracles, which
will one day shout 'Hosanna to the Son of David!' and on the
next shout 'Crucify him!' He is challenging the lazy sentimen-
tality, the shallowness, of their curiosity. Time and again he
warns off those who might be romanticising the call, who have
not faced for themselves the need for total commitment (cf. the
rich young ruler, Matt. 19:21, 22). So he is not telling them to
be cautious: he is telling them to be truthful with themselves
about what it is they are contemplating.

So, in metaphoric mode, the life of discipleship may be lived
at humble 'farmer' level or leadership 'kingly' level, but it will
always involve decision-making which must be realistic, for it
will be life-changing. Ambitious enterprise, spiritually, may
result in humiliating failure, and ridicule, or destruction and
'exile' (exclusion?) not simply for oneself but for those one
leads. And one is reminded instantly of Peter, declaring, 'Lord,
I am ready to go to prison with you and to death' (Luke 22:33):
Peter, that is, 'starting to build a tower' for which he has not
fully worked out the resources. Peter, 'going to war against
evil' without truthfully assessing what it will demand.

We may go further. The 'resources' are the key. With hindsight
we recognise Peter failed (just as when he walked on the water)
when he lost total reliance on his Lord: when he saw him a
prisoner and therefore unable – it would seem – to offer him
the resource that he needed. Jesus himself spoke of the 'twelve
legions of angels' he could have summoned had that seemed
right (Matt. 26:53). 'Troops', therefore, are not the ultimate issue;
but an appraisal of the appropriate resources which are properly on hand, those of God as well as of man.

And this brings us to our own reading of the stories. The
young Christian community would see them as illustrations of
the need for total commitment, whatever the cost. Standing
in the light of 2,000 years of Christian grace, *we* are able to
speak also of how the resources to sustain that commitment

must be found, not from our own exaggerated notion of spiritual adequacy, but from that which God supplies through Christ. For the enemy that comes against us will always have twice the power we ourselves wield, twenty thousand to our ten. What we have to establish is whether we are tapped into the resources beyond ourselves, which will enable us to avoid the ignominy of 'suing for peace'. In the end, sitting down and taking careful thought about that could indeed be a matter of life and death.

'The Two Houses' (Matt. 7:24–27; Luke 6;47–49)

Our first pair of micro-parables, 'The Treasure', and 'The Pearl', underlined the need for total commitment in response to the discerned moment. Our second pair, 'The Tower Builder', and 'The King Planning War', emphasised the need for that commitment to be realistically appraised and resourced. Our third 'pair' is contained within the one parable: the story of 'The Two Houses'. This is another vignette, this time of the contrast between the one who does, and the one who does not, act on the words of Jesus. So this is taking us a stage further: from 'recognition of the need for commitment', through 'establishing the resources available', to 'acting on that commitment'. How does the parable of 'The Two Houses' develop this?

It appears as a part of Jesus' general teaching in both Matthew and Luke. Its immediate context, in both, is a discourse about the difference between the *appearance* of good and its reality: in Matthew the image is of 'false prophets', and in Luke of the 'good person' out of the 'good treasure of the heart' producing 'good'. This is summarised, in Matthew, in the disturbing comment: 'Not everyone who says to me "Lord, Lord" will enter the kingdom of heaven: but only one who does the will of my father in heaven' (7:21). In Luke this becomes even sharper: 'Why do you call me "Lord, Lord" and do not do what I tell you?' (6:46). There follows the parable. After it, Matthew records the crowd as 'astounded at his teaching, for he taught them as one having authority and not as their scribes'.

This is our clue into the dynamic of this story. For Jesus begins each part of the story with a direct link into 'obedience'

or 'disobedience': 'Everyone then who hears these words of
mine and acts on them . . . Everyone who hears these words
of mine and does not act on them . . .' The first is 'like a wise
man'; the second is 'like a foolish man' (Matthew).

'Obedience' or 'disobedience' to what? Or rather, to whom?
The reason that the people were 'astonished' becomes very
clear. For this is the prophetic voice, speaking in the name of
God himself, with a pure anger rejecting the hypocrisy of false
praise and disordered lives. It is resonant of God's direct
address to his people through so many stages of disobedience
recorded in the Old Testament:

> I hate, I despise your festivals,
>   and I take no delight in your solemn assemblies.
> Even though you offer me your burnt
>   offerings and grain offerings,
>   I will not accept them . . .
> Take away from me the noise of your songs,
>   I will not listen to the melody of your harps.
> But let justice roll down like waters,
>   and righteousness
>   like an ever-flowing stream.
>
>   (Amos 5:21, 22a, 23, 24)

We are reminded that continually, in the Old Testament, to be
'foolish' is to live as though there were no God. The 'foolish
man' of the parable of 'The Two Houses', therefore, is living
'as though there were no God' – godlessly. So the teaching of
which this story is the culmination focuses everything that is
said of living as 'children of the Most High' (Luke 6:35) in
doing, or not doing, *the words of Jesus*. It follows that the word
of Jesus is the word of God himself. No greater authority could
be claimed.

The story
We are now in a position to look closely at the actual story. The
realistic metonymic details are clear, and almost identical in the
two gospel versions. The two houses are given no external
differences. The distinction between them is *where* they are built,
and *how* they are built. One is built 'on rock' (Matt. 7:24): that
is (Luke 6:48), its builder 'dug deeply and laid the foundation

on rock'. The other is built 'on sand' (Matt. 7:26): that is, 'without a foundation' (Luke 6:49a). What is in view here is almost certainly a structure erected on a sandy *wadi*. There follows a vivid description of the storm rising, with rain, and consequent floods, their power heightened by the 'winds that blew and beat on that house' (Matt. 7:25). These vivid and realistic details become almost cantatory, almost choric, repeated as they are: 'The rain fell, and the floods came, and the winds blew and beat against that house' (Matt. 7:27). This is metonymic realism both of the detail of the natural world, and how Palestinians experienced it regularly: and also of the classic storyteller, building up the tension through this almost irresistible, unavoidable, piling of threat on threat. (Luke's version is much less dramatic but just as authentic: 'and when a flood arose, the river burst against that house . . .')

That there *is* a metaphoric mode to the parable has been indicated by the introduction: that 'doers' and 'non-doers' of Christ's words are 'like' the 'wise' builder, or the 'foolish' builder. But the image of the 'flood' takes us directly into the metaphor. For what is being described is a deluge. And the Deluge is one of the great stories of the Old Testament in which metonymic and metaphoric modes cross to express the developing relationship of God with his people. The 'wise' – Noah and his family – survive the dreadful flood because they hear the words of God, and do them. The people amongst whom Noah lives do not 'hear and do', and are swept away. 'Justice has rolled down like waters . . .'

Moreover, behind this evocation of the flood of Judgement sweeping away the disobedient in the past, lies another echo: that of a prophet as familiar to Christ's listeners as the story of the Deluge. Isaiah 28:16 and 17 runs:

> Therefore, thus says the Lord God,
> See, I am laying in Zion a foundation stone,
>   a tested stone,
> a precious cornerstone, a sure foundation:
>   'One who trusts will not panic.'
> And I will make justice the line,
>   and righteousness the plummet;
> hail will sweep away the refuge of lies,
>   and waters will overwhelm the shelter.

For Christ's first listeners to this story, therefore, it has the double impact of the homely concrete illustration, something they have all seen at some time in the village's history; and the powerful metaphor of 'Flood' on the one hand: 'waters overwhelm[ing] the shelter'; and security on the other: the 'sure foundation' of 'trust'; 'one who trusts will not panic'. The quotation from Isaiah invites 'trust' in God. The parable invites, in parallel, 'trust' in Jesus. The kind of trust which issues in obedient action.

The gospel editors, particularly Matthew, while maintaining this thrust to the story, add more sharply the notion of judgement: 'I never knew you; go away from me, you evil-doers' is Matthew's immediate preface to the story. So it is the Noachic Flood which is primary as an echo here.

And how does the story address _us_? In spite of our technology we remain as a human race vulnerable to natural disaster, and our TV screens have from time to time brought us to the scene of appalling destruction and suffering. So the metonymic pattern of the parable still addresses us. Its metaphoric mode, too, challenges us as a Church as it once challenged the Pharisees – 'I despise your festivals! Let justice roll down like waters.' 'Why do you call me "Lord, Lord", and do not do what I tell you?' 'He who hears these words of mine and does not act on them . . .' The Church is no less open to the Judgement of the waters than the Pharisees were.

But the other side of this, of course, is the promise of security for the 'wise' who hear, and act: who are the children of Isaiah, 'free of panic' because the 'one who trusts' rests on a 'sure foundation'. Whether within the Church or without, the parables offer the same opportunity for ultimate security. Commitment – that is, total trust. And obedience: that is, saying 'Lord, Lord' – and _doing_ what he tells us.

'The Untrustworthy Manager' (Luke 16:1–8)

Of all Jesus' parables this must be the most obscure, in the sense that its plain meaning seems self-contradictory, and in any case alien to the 'life of the Kingdom of heaven' as we find Jesus declaring it in his other stories, his teaching generally, his great 'works', and his death and Resurrection. The problem arises chiefly near the parable's end, in the comment, 'and his master commended the dishonest manager because he had acted shrewdly, for the children of this age are more shrewd in dealing with their own generation than the children of light' (16:8). Many commentators have taken this to mean that Jesus himself was saying there was something commendable about the manager's actions, something we could usefully copy. Most agree, however, that there is no single clear interpretation to the story, but several possible ones.

I want to suggest that the clue to a less strained reading of the parable rests on the nature of its actual audience – to whom was it addressed? The opening words are clear enough: 'Then Jesus said to his disciples' (16:1a). But if we look at the conclusion of the story, we find it is rounded off with a number of sayings all of which relate in some way to issues of wealth, the pursuit of riches, and the choice to be made between these and the service of God. (At first sight it looks as though Luke as editor has collected these together in relation to the story simply because the phrases 'dishonest wealth', 'true riches', appear in them.) These 'sayings' are then followed by the comment, 'The Pharisees, *who were lovers of money*, heard all this, and they ridiculed him' (16:14).

Now if we look at what Luke has put as immediately preceding this parable, with, indeed, no intermission at all, we find that it is the story of 'The Prodigal Son, the Loving Father, and the Elder Brother': and *that* story was told in the presence of 'grumbling' Pharisees and scribes who were disapproving of the unacceptable nature of many attracted by Jesus' teaching, for 'all the tax-collectors and sinners were coming near to listen to him' (15:1, 2).

So in setting out the telling of the story of 'The Untrustworthy Manager', Luke is clearly envisaging the Pharisees as it were 'listening in', or 'eavesdropping', as Jesus talks with his apparent audience – in the case of 'The Prodigal Son', the social rejects, in the case of 'The Untrustworthy Manager', the disciples. It is, so to speak, a 'trialogue' which is taking place: a story which has a message for the immediate audience and an even sharper message for those known to be listening, but distantly, as refusing engagement. If we then take Jesus' response to the Pharisees' 'ridicule' of what he has been saying, a response with which Luke rounds off both the account of

'The Untrustworthy Manager' and the sayings which follow it, we find we have a 'code-breaker', a key to the *metaphoric* mode both of the story and of the sayings which follow it: 'So he said to them, "You are those who justify yourselves in the sight of others; but God knows your hearts; for what is prized by human beings is an abomination in the sight of God"' (16:15).

The story
So now we may turn to the story. In metonymic terms it is a situation readily recognisable to Christ's listeners. A rich estate, with an owner much away – possibly even a foreign owner? – and an estate manager who in his master's absence has complete control over everything. But dissatisfaction against the manager has been rising, and one day 'charges were brought' to the owner that his manager had been 'squandering' his property. (This could mean anything from living the high life at the estate's expense, holding lavish parties for local society, to not handling the estate funds in such a way as to bring in its proper profit.) Again, such managers would be familiar to Jesus' listeners, and no doubt a local target for gossip and criticism.

So the manager is called to account – literally. He is told that he is sacked, and that the estate records are to be handed over. A delightfully vivid satirical thumbnail sketch follows, of the wily manager pondering how best to retrieve whatever is retrievable. He is not of a physical constitution that would support him working in the fields as a hired labourer – which would in any case be socially beneath him. And he could not bear the humiliation of begging. Yet somehow he *must maintain his social position* – so that 'people may welcome' him 'into their homes'. Which is all he needs, for his skills are clearly those of a conman. The way to do it, he decides, is to put them in his personal debt: connive with them so that they do not have to pay their debts to his master. So he 'summons' his master's debtors one by one – note that he is in the dominant position here, still, able to 'summon' the very people it is part of his design to get to receive *him* when his fall comes. He gets *them* to change, in their own writing, the sums due. They are huge. Either these are outstanding rents, or debts accumulated for goods received; or – an interesting suggestion from one commentator – they are interest due on money from the estate which the manager has (illicitly?) loaned out. It is very high interest, so he would be planning to keep at least part of it for himself. If, however, he remits half the interest, his master gets his capital back together with a fair return. The manager has lost his personal profit, but the owner can pin nothing actually dishonest on him. And by making the debtors *themselves* alter the debt documents, he can always hope that either nothing will be noticed, because the handwriting is the same throughout, or, if it is noticed, it will be the debtors who are held responsible, since it is *their* handwriting which has altered the debt.

The owner 'commended' his manager: in other words he recognised that faced with disaster he has found a way to survive in the kind of world he wanted to survive in. By such 'commendation' the master is not necessarily giving ultimate approval, but appreciating in a thoroughly Middle Eastern way the wiliness of a survivor. (We could, of course, always keep open the possibility that the *master* is as 'bent' as the manager, and appreciates his roguery!)

Two 'sayings' have then been added; one, that 'the children of this age are more shrewd in dealing with their own generation than the children of light'. And the second, 'And I tell you, make friends for yourselves by means of dishonest wealth, so that when it is gone, they may welcome you into the eternal homes' (16:8b, and 9). In the light of the sayings that immediately follow, this latter comment looks as though, stripped of its awkward phrasing, it simply means, 'Show you can be trusted with the riches which are "dishonest" i.e., worldly wealth – so that in eternity your trustworthiness will serve you a home "with the angels" – i.e., with God.' The earlier of the two comments has curious phrasing – 'children of light', for instance, is a quite rare phrase used primarily of a religious sect. It looks as though it means that 'the children of this generation' – i.e., this worldly generation now alive, know how to deal with the fiscal catastrophes imposed on them by their fellows better than those 'who have come out from among them'. We may see how far this is applicable when we have read the story in its metaphoric mode.

The metaphor
For if the words addressed so sharply to the Pharisees are indeed the key to the story, then it is *not* ultimately about

wealth and how to handle it at all – though it is clear the early Church read it, and the sayings that followed, in this way. Rather, it is about the 'untrustworthy management' by the religious leaders of *God's estate*. 'Charges' are laid against them – by the very fact of the coming of Jesus? – that they are 'squandering' God's property: the souls of his people Israel, and therefore of the world to whom that people should be a blessing. So charged, the instant reaction of the Pharisees is how 'to justify themselves in the sight of others' (16:15) (so that 'people may welcome' them 'into their homes'? – cf. Luke 14:12). Hence, having laid intolerable burdens on God's debtors, they are prepared to connive at ways of getting round this (e.g. Mark 7:11–13) in order to go on being honoured amongst their generation. Indeed they show shrewdness in political and worldly affairs; 'but God knows [their] hearts; for what is prized by human beings is an abomination in the sight of God' (Luke 16:15).

The teaching sayings which immediately follow the parable, and which, with the parable, are 'ridiculed' by the Pharisees, lend substance to this reading of the story in metaphoric mode. For the emphasis throughout is on 'faithfulness'. If they are not 'faithful with another's' – God's? – then 'who will give [them] what is [their] own?' 'Whoever is faithful in little is faithful in much.' In the end, therefore, the parable is about 'faithfulness' – commitment – outworking in action, in a precise and particular example, that of the religious leaders charged with the manage-ment of God's good estate, the people of Israel. What has mattered to them most? Being received in people's houses, or faithful stewarding?

And how does it address us? For the same questions address us, both in the Church and beyond it. Do we in any sense 'squander' our Lord's estate, the souls of his children? Though the form of that squandering may be different from that which Jesus attacked, is its essence any different? And when we are challenged on this, what is our reply? To render our account penitently and truthfully, and ask for mercy? Or to try to fudge and compromise, and retain our public role and social acceptability? Difficult as it is, the parable of 'The Untrust-worthy Manager' questions us as sharply as once it did the Pharisees. It leads us on, by its picture of the manager, unre-pentant, trying to cover his tracks and maintain what he regards as 'his position', to those other, darker parables of almost total disobedience. So it is to them that we must now turn.

11 The Parables of 'The Two Sons', 'The Usurping Tenants', 'The Merciless Servant' and 'The Rich Man and Lazarus the Beggar'

THIS IS THE DARKEST part of our reading of the parables. For, of course, the challenge to commitment and consequent obedience when the moment of decisive encounter is discerned – encounter with the God of sovereign grace – always leaves open the possibility of non-commitment; more, of deliberate and chosen *dis*-obedience. The stories we shall read in this chapter all describe the dreadful reality of this option. And, apart from the first parable, they are unrelieved in their choice. What we are brought face to face with is human wickedness. Not simply the disobedience we find dangerously easy to distance from ourselves, that of the religious leaders of a particular nation at a particular time, whom Jesus is castigating. Nor even the wider but still distanced alienation of a particular nation. Rather, we are brought face to face with humanity in general. Ultimately, then, we are brought face to face with ourselves. For these are stories about *us*, quite as powerfully as they are stories about life in Israel at the time of the Incarnation, or even about the history of that nation's relationship with God.

'The Two Sons' (Matt. 21:28–32) and 'The Usurping Tenants' (Mark 12:1–12; Matt. 21:33–41; Luke 20:9–18)

Our first two stories must to some extent be taken together, because though 'The Two Sons' appears only in Matthew, it appears in the same context as, and is interpolated immediately prior to, the parable of 'The Usurping Tenants', which appears in all three of the synoptic gospels, and is given virtually the same context in each. (It is worth noting that 'The Usurping Tenants' is one of only four parables which appear in all these three gospels; of these, two are micro-parables – 'The Mustard Seed' and 'The Budding Fig-Tree' – and only one is a 'full-length' parable, that of 'The Sower'. We may therefore fairly assume both the accreditation and the importance to those who heard it of this story of human wickedness.)

The context

The context of these stories is vital to at least our first reading of them, for all three gospel writers 'place' the moment as in the immediate wake of the crucial question the 'chief priests and elders of the people' address to Jesus as he is in the Temple, 'teaching' (Matthew) and 'telling them the good news' (Luke), or simple 'walking' (Mark). That question is the vital one, which *must* be asked by those of spiritual integrity who genuinely want the truth, and *may* be asked as a clever political device by those who see Jesus as the enemy for whom, for 'righteousness' sake – or that of their own status – traps must be dug. The question is one that is to be asked by the honest seeker in every generation, including our own: 'By what authority are you doing these things, and who gave you that authority?' (Matt. 21:23b; Mark 11:28; Luke 20:2).

This is 'crossover' language. For metonymically it could simply refer to local authorisation for Jesus' immediate actions and teaching. He has already turned out the money-changers, healed, and taught in the Temple, within the first couple of days of his arrival in Jerusalem riding on an ass, attended by the Hosanna-singing crowd. But what authority has he been given, and who by, for instance to *teach* there in the Temple? It is a task requiring certain specific qualifications achieved by long study, not least because it involves detailed knowledge of law. He therefore needs either formal study qualifications or formal accreditation, or both. The same, but with even more force, could with absolute propriety be asked of his dramatic actions in 'cleaning up' the Temple: even if there were some commercial abuse here, who gave *him* the right to deal with it? One can hear in the very language of today that kind of questioning. The question, that is, can arise, with justification, *honestly*: out of a genuine desire to know the truth about this particular set of circumstances. In other words in its metonymic dimensions it is not necessarily primarily a theological question but an administrative one which can be fairly asked. Where does he 'fit' in the management structures of the Temple – seen as the religious institution which is the centre and key to the whole of the Jewish social structure, and therefore to be guarded against improper intrusion?

But of course, in its metaphorical mode, it is a profoundly theological question; and because the Temple as a religious institution is in the end about expressing the centrality of God in the life of the nation, that *theological* dimension lies behind all the administrative and management questions. So it is to the question in its metaphorical, theological mode that Jesus responds.

He responds with another question; and offers, if they will tell him their answer to it, to reply in kind to the question they have asked him. *His* question is in fact the same question they have asked him, but this time as referring to his forerunner, John the Baptist. 'Did the baptism of John come from heaven, or was it of human origin?' (Matt. 21:25; Mark 11:30; Luke 20:4). The question is in the theological, metaphoric mode, though metonymic consequences are involved. In effect, Christ's interlocutors are being asked of John the Baptist the question they asked of Jesus: 'By what authority did John baptise? Was he divinely accredited, or was this merely a human phenomenon?'

Ultimately they give the answer, 'We do not know' (Matt. 21:27; Mark 11:33; Luke 20:7). And they are telling the truth. They do not know. And if, even with hindsight, they are unable to discern God in the work of John the Baptist, then there is no point at all in Jesus attempting to convey to them the reality of his own divine authority. For they simply cannot entertain it with understanding and assent.

So part of the point of this context is to indicate what the two parables then go on to explore, a complete inability to enter the mindset (soul-set?) which would help recognition of the nature of Christ's authority. But we are given more than this. For besides the *conclusion* to which they come, that they 'do not know' whether God's authority rested on John the Baptist, we are given the *workings* of their minds by which they reach that conclusion. And we are to see the way in which they reason precisely reflected in the way the 'Usurping Tenants' reason in the parable.

For their reasoning is dominated wholly by self-interest. They do not inquire of each other what may actually be the truth about the authority authenticating John the Baptist. Rather they 'argued with one another' about how best to handle the question *politically*.

If they declared that God had authorised John, then, they feared, they would be challenged as to why they did not 'believe him', i.e., take to their hearts his message, to repent and to prepare for the coming great moment of encounter with God. There is no hint that they wish they *had* believed him, or felt in honesty they could not. Only a weighing of 'political' consequence in what they clearly saw as a *political* struggle with Jesus for honour and respect among the people. To have missed discerning a prophet, a true contemporary prophet sent of God, would be to admit a profound and disastrous failure as religious leaders. Therefore they could betray no hint at all that this might have been the case. Their own pride would not allow it.

But the alternative was equally dangerous. For to suggest in the hearing of the crowd pressing round them that John was merely self-authenticating, that he was not 'sent of God', was to invite a riot, the crowd, if not the leaders, having discerned the spiritual authority that was John's. Again this clearly led to no self-questioning on the part of the leaders, merely a contempt for the naïveté of the crowd. But it meant that only one answer was left them: a temporising 'we do not know' which attempted to imply the question was far too complex and profound to be answered by a simple affirmative.

And it is because this is their mode of thinking, as well as the plain fact that they genuinely 'do not know', which makes it impossible for Jesus to give them any answer about the authority invested in himself. Instead, since they cannot meet his conditions for response, he briefly indicates he will not tell them of that authority: but then goes on, in the Matthew version of events, to tell two stories directly applicable to the issue of authority. One is that of 'The Two Sons'. The other is that of 'The Usurping Tenants'.

'The Two Sons'

This is a brief, very simple, very pointed parable, whose metonymic detail is kept to a minimum. The owner of a vineyard is introduced to us as a father with two sons. (Indeed, we know him as a father before we know him as a vineyard owner.)

He asks the first to go and work in his vineyard that day, and gets the absolute reply, 'I will not.' But afterwards the boy changes his mind, and goes. Exactly the reverse happens with the second. Perhaps the only detail extra that we ought to note is the address of the second to his father, 'I go, sir' (*Kurie*, 'lord'). So one is rude yet ultimately obedient; the other is polite to the point of obsequiousness, but ultimately disobedient.

In the instantly familiar metonymic world of parents and children, the point is made emphatically, because this is a rhetorical story, a 'question' parable. The key issue, the only point that matters, rests in the concluding question: 'Which of the two did the will of his father?' (Matt. 21:31a). There is only one possible reply: 'The first.' The religious leaders give him that reply, guardedly. Jesus' comment, in response, is our bridge into the metaphorical mode of the parable, and its profounder meaning. For he picks up the *theological* dimension of the discussion recorded as preceding the story, about the divine authority undergirding both John and himself. John, he says, came to them 'in the way of righteousness' but they did not 'believe' him: that is, allow themselves to be warned by him of the coming encounter with God, and prepare themselves penitently for it. Yet the 'outsiders' – tax-gatherers and prostitutes – *did* believe him: responded with penitence and longing. And even then the religious leaders did not 'change their minds', but remained sceptical. *Therefore* those outsiders 'are going into the Kingdom of God' ahead of their leaders. For they have recognised the authority of God and obeyed it. With their whole way of life, to that point, they had seemed to say to the Father, on his call to work obediently in his vineyard, 'I will not.' Certainly their mode of life would not only 'seem' but 'be' the epitome of disobedience to God by the standards of the religious leaders. But afterwards, when they 'believed' in John, they 'changed their minds', and obeyed God's command. Meanwhile the religious leaders had been saying to their God the equivalent of 'I go, sir', yet remained inactive and uncommitted in that way of life *of the heart* for which God looked.

But the metaphoric mode of the parable takes us further. For its very essence is about 'doing the will of the father'. The issue therefore of the authority which lay behind John's baptism, like the issue of the authority which invested Jesus, lay in that simple question: 'Was he doing the will of the Father?' What is

their 'authority'? To have been told to 'go to work in the vineyard', and to have obeyed. Both Jesus and John have done this:
so they have the authority of the Father's command and their
own obedience. And because the outsiders have heard them,
and responded to them gladly with obedient hearts, even they,
like the recalcitrant son of the parable, have been 'covered by'
the authority vested first in John, then in Jesus. In Luke's gospel,
at another point (7:29), we find this very judgement amplified:

> *And all the people who heard this, including the tax collectors,
> acknowledged the justice of God [or: praised God], because they
> had been baptized with John's baptism. But by refusing to be
> baptized by him, the Pharisees and the lawyers rejected God's
> purpose for themselves.*

How may the two modes of this parable address us today?
'Authority', certainly in our Western culture, is a conceptual
football, kicked about by individuals playing to different sets
of rules or none at all. Yet there is a widespread search for
the authentic word of God, accredited by a genuine authority
discerned as *of God*. How, among the siren voices, may that
be discerned? Can this little parable help us?

The test of the genuineness of that divine authority seems to
be, quite simply, not in covering God with word-play or even
worshipping him in resonant phrases, but in 'doing the will of
the Father'. So for us the criterion must surely be whether this
or that calls us to such a readiness for the moment of encounter
with God, that we penitently prepare ourselves for that
encounter, and *with our hearts* 'do the will of the Father'. Not
so much talking about him, that is, or even talking about
obeying him; but actually, in the teeth of our loudly declared
earlier refusals, *doing* it. And we are only able to discern
'authority' in the call to such a life if the one sounding the call
is himself or herself visibly 'doing the will of the Father'. For
in the end scepticism is overcome by the reality of 'goodness',
unless that scepticism is invested, as it was in the case of these
long-ago religious leaders, with self-interest and fear of threat
to the *status quo* of their *own* authority.

'The Usurping Tenants'

The story which follows, in Matthew, and which by itself in
Mark and Luke is used by Jesus to illustrate this issue of
'authority', appears in almost identical detail in all three
accounts. The only variants are that in Luke the preliminary
details of preparing the vineyard are less fully sketched in (and
this is not without significance, as we shall see); and the number
of servants in Matthew is rather different – they come in groups,
rather than singly.

The metonymic detail of this story is important, because
without it we should find it an unlikely, if pleasingly dramatic
tale. In fact much of it would be instantly recognisable to Jesus'
listeners without much explanation; indeed it is possible that,
like so many of his parables, it related to an actual incident.
The vineyard has been established, carefully, by an owner who,
once it has been properly prepared, will be an absentee land-
lord. He might well have been one of the many foreign
landowners whose grip on the land provided a background of
angry resentment out of which movements like the Zealots
found their support. Nevertheless, the estate is properly and
legally his, and he has invested labour, skill and care in it. The
vineyard is not only 'planted' in ground properly prepared, but
'fenced round' and a wine press dug out (usually with a rock
base channelled in preparation). The 'fencing round' is not only
to shelter the young plants, but for security. In the same cause
a 'watchtower' is erected, a vital precaution particularly at
harvest time. When the owner goes away, renting out the vineyard to tenants, it is with good reason: for three years there
will be no profitable harvest from the vines, and in the fourth
year, under Jewish religious law, most of what constitutes the
'first-fruits' of the vineyard will go in religious offering. Nevertheless, it is not so unprofitable a project for the tenants in those
four years as it might seem, for the vines are widely spaced
when planted, and between them (as we saw in the parable of
'The Barren Fig-Tree') other crops can be grown. The owner
would expect a fairly nominal rent for these first four years,
but from the sale of that other produce certainly some return
should have been forthcoming.

It is not clear, therefore, whether the clause 'when the harvest
time had come' refers to this interim 'alternative' harvest, or to

the first year – i.e., the fifth – when the owner could look for real profit. And it does not really matter, except that if it refers to the latter it underlines how long the owner has had to wait for any real return, and how long also the tenants have got used to thinking of the vineyard as their own.

The owner's establishing of his legal ownership of the vineyard will depend on two things: his title deeds, and his ability to prove that he has claimed rent each year. Hence the importance of his servants being sent to claim, however nominally, a rent for the place. But 'slaves' could not legally be witnesses, so that their evidence of attempts to collect rent would be useless. Hence, eventually, it would be necessary for someone of legal status to go for the rent: either the owner himself or, if he was too busy, a member of the family: his son, perhaps. The detail of the 'son' being sent, therefore, is of *metonymic* significance initially: and it does not necessarily have any theological significance in the metonymic world of the parable. It is only when we come to the parable's *metaphorical* mode that it could take on profound meaning.

If this is the 'only' son – the heir – then the legal calculations of the tenants are not as wild as they seem. For there are two possibilities: first, that the busy and absent owner will simply wash his hands of the vineyard, as not being worth his trouble. Or, second, that even if he tries to reclaim it, he will have difficulty proving his claim. If he abandons it, then unclaimed land can indeed, under the law, be taken by those who invest it – a sort of squatter's right. So the reasoning of the tenants is not baseless.

But of course they have not allowed for the other metonymic element in the story; for what could belong more naturally and integratedly to *this* world than an owner's wrath at dispossession of a carefully prepared vineyard, and insulting and aggressive behaviour to his servants; and a father's rage at the killing of his son and heir? These are such basic human responses in the kind of situation sketched out, that Jesus can safely ask the rhetorical question, 'Now when the owner of the vineyard comes, what will he do to those tenants?' The answer is unhesitating: 'He will come and destroy those tenants and give the vineyard to others' (Mark, Luke): 'He will put those wretches to a miserable death, and lease the vineyard to other tenants who will give him the produce at harvest time' (Matt.).

Thus far the metonymic world within which the story operates: familiar enough to Christ's listeners. But the *metaphoric* mode would in this case be accessible as well, because of their familiarity with a passage from Isaiah bearing striking similarity to the beginning of the story. Isaiah 5:1b-4 runs as follows:

> My beloved had a vineyard
>   on a very fertile hill.
> He dug it, and cleared it of stones,
>   and planted it with choice vines;
> he built a watchtower in the midst of it,
>   and hewed out a wine vat in it;
> he expected it to yield grapes
>   but it yielded wild grapes.
> And now, inhabitants of Jerusalem
>   and people of Judah,
> judge between me and my vineyard.
> What more was there to do for my vineyard
>   that I have not done in it?
> When I expected it to yield grapes,
>   why did it yield wild grapes?

This is why Luke's version of the parable is less strong, metaphorically: it does not access as the other two versions do this complaint by God against his people which is part of the material Jesus is clearly drawing on for the purposes of the story. And now we are in a position to begin to examine the thrust of the story as we discover it when metonymic and metaphoric modes cross.

Reading the story

The 'ways into' the metaphoric mode of the story are first, this background of Isaiah's metaphor of the vineyard; second, the context out of which the story comes, the issue of Christ's own investment of authority; third, the introduction in Mark and Luke of the phrase 'beloved son' (Mark 12:6a: 'He had still one other, a beloved son'); and fourth, Christ's comments at the end of the story (again virtually identical in all three accounts). These refer to the scriptural quotation (from Ps. 118:22, 23) concerning the builder's rejected stone which has become the keystone, and which will be a means of judgement. To this

Matthew adds an actual application of the story: 'Therefore I tell you, the Kingdom of God will be taken away from you and given to a people that produces the fruits of the Kingdom.' All three accounts conclude with the religious leaders' recognition that in the parables 'he was speaking about them'; and consequently, they long to seize him but are yet constrained by their fears as to how the crowd would react, 'because they regarded him as a prophet'.

We may begin, however, with none of these, but with the tenants' own reflections as they are faced with the owner's final emissary. They are simply described in terms of *action* in relation to the previous messengers, the servants, whom they 'insult', 'beat', 'stone' and 'kill'. Remembering the fence and the watch-tower, what we have here is a determined use of the defences *against the owner himself* and his representatives. In other words he is betrayed not by any of the exterior forces against which he has set up his defences, but by the enemy within. With the coming of the son and heir we are offered some of the tenants' reflections, and they are the clue to the motive behind the previous actions. After all it is possible – just – that the owner's servants had been thought to be imposters trying to find a way through the defences (the version of this parable in the *Gospel of Thomas* actually has the owner saying 'They may not have known my servant'). Their discussion together on seeing the son and heir refuted this. 'This is the heir; come, let us kill him and get his inheritance.' This is now a plain case of usurpation: they think of the vineyard as 'theirs' and they are prepared to take any vile action to secure it.

The analogy should not be missed, with the anxious discussion among the religious leaders concerning the politic response to Jesus' question about the authority invested in John the Baptist's baptism. In each case there is an utter refusal to 'give ground', to yield in any way to an invasion by truth or reality which would challenge their own position. They too have become 'usurpers', taking to themselves as of their own right an authority to which they will allow no challenge.

So how might the story have been heard in Jesus' time? The metaphoric mode approached through the 'Isaiah' parallel would lead them to think of it as a story about the nation as a whole, for that was the thrust of Isaiah's material. But here it is those responsible for running the vineyard who are being reproached, and the owner is complaining not about the nature of the produce of the vineyard, 'wild grapes instead of good grapes', but against the produce being kept back from him, kept for themselves, by those in charge. So this must certainly have been heard, as the story was told, as an attack on the 'husbandmen' of God's vineyard, the religious leaders. Thus the material succeeding the story, in each of the three accounts, where the leaders recognise the parable as about themselves, does not sound like an interpretative gloss by the early Church, but a dramatic note about the rising hate and fear of the religious leaders.

But in what sense could the parable seem to have any force against them? What have they done that is in any way like the action of the tenants? They have kept the goodness of God for themselves and their kind, and not freely returned it to God for his purposes – in this case for those 'outsiders' for whom they have such contempt. John the Baptist and Jesus have been emissaries asking that God's 'rent' be paid – that the produce of the religious life of the nation may go where he wishes it to go, in his own purposes. And they have refused, believing that all the sacred 'property' of God's relationship with his people is properly *theirs* to hold and allocate. Hence they are usurpers in the vineyard which is the Kingdom, and it will be taken from them and given to a people who will produce for God the right fruit.

This takes us from how the story would first be heard, to how the early Church heard it. For this focus on 'produce' which under the new dispensation will be given to the owner at harvest time, as well as the reference to a 'people that produces the fruit of the kingdom' – both of which are extra details in Matthew – shift the focus *away* from the usurping wickedness of the 'tenants' to the need to 'produce fruits' for the owner. At root, these two interpretations join: for the real wickedness of the tenants was that they no longer recognised the owner as having ultimate claim: in metaphoric terms, those responsible for the religious life of Israel no longer recognised that ultimately they must answer, not to each other, or the law, but to God. Producing at the right time his 'rental' of fruit was a metaphoric symbol of this. But for the young Church, faced with the need for waiting longer than they had first thought for the 'coming' of the 'owner', and 'harvest time', the emphasis shifts on to the need to concentrate on being 'fruitful vines', ready for the Harvest, the Last Day. For them the son of the story has become the 'beloved' and 'the only' son – neither of them Messianic terms the original listeners would have recognised. Hence, fruitfulness till Judgement Day is underlined by the later reference to the neglected or rejected 'stone' which is now the 'keystone' and which, in the ruin of Judgement Day, will smash down on those who have not acknowledged the 'beloved Son'.

And how does the parable address *us*? Given our current ecological concerns, very powerfully on at least one level. For we could read this as a story nearly parallel to that of the creation story in Genesis where, put in as stewards of a lovely estate, we have chosen to think of it as a matter for our own disposal only, with no sense of it as a vineyard whose produce is in debt to God.

But it goes deeper than this, of course, for that searching question of 'authority' underlies the whole story. In brief, those currently in occupation of God's 'estate' are not its owners, are *never* its owners, in whatever culture or century or sect or Christian belief we find ourselves. Any authority any of us hold in God's estate is entirely one of tenancy, and it is answerable always to the authority of heaven. Hence it is vital that for the period of our own tenancy we are alert to, ready for, and *open to* the emissaries of God the rightful owner, who will make demands on us that are appropriate to our tenancy. Otherwise we may slip into habits of spiritual usurpation which do not recognise the authority of the One who comes: do not recognise it in the Teller of this tale, do not recognise it in his many voices and messengers in the 2,000 years since he told it. And thus find ourselves, asked to discern whether this or that voice be of 'heaven or of men', in panic distancing ourselves and replying – lest we be asked for some painful delivering up of fruit – of God's very Messenger himself, that 'we do not know'.

'The Merciless Servant' (Matt. 18:23–35)

This is perhaps the darkest parable in the whole Bible, because it is metonymically a story of extraordinary magnanimity experienced and then end-stopped: not allowed to flow through the one receiving it, but wrested to one person as applicable only to himself. In metaphoric mode, it is about the most important gift in the world, the forgiveness of God; and of what its operation should be allowed to be, and of the fearful consequences when that operation is wilfully curtailed.

The story arises when Peter famously asks about the proper limits of forgiveness. 'If my brother sins against me, how often should I forgive him? As many as seven times?' Jesus' reply, 'Not seven times, but, I tell you, seventy times seven' is then followed in Matthew's account by this story which thus links 'the kingdom of heaven' with the activity of forgiving: 'For this reason the kingdom of heaven may be compared to a king . . .' In Luke's version of this conversation no story appears, but, rather endearingly, the disciples respond to the demand for such total magnanimity with the dismayed interjection, 'Lord, increase our faith!'

So it is clear that 'forgiving', 'the kingdom', and 'faith' are all somehow interlinked. The story expresses, that is, their conjunction.

The story
The parable has the beautifully balanced structure so characteristic of Jesus' longer stories. A situation is set out: that of the king receiving the accounts of the kingdom and calling in outstanding debts. Chief among these is one huge debt, which the debtor cannot pay; so, in law, he, his wife, children and possessions must all be sold towards payment. But then there is the first development: he pleads for mercy, the king is filled with pity, and releases him, forgiving him 'all that debt'. Therefore the relationship between them is changed: this man has been transformed by the king's mercy from debtor to 'honest' servant once more. He can take up his life again – a life which has been returned to him through forgiveness.

So the next development is the first action he takes in this newly returned life. As he leaves the court of the king he meets one who is, in turn, indebted to *him*, though for a comparatively minute account. There follows an exact replay of what has gone before, with, this time, the first debtor in the role of creditor. But he is untouched by pity when his debtor pleads for mercy, and enforces instead the full distraint of the law.

So the climax lies in the reactions to this of those around.

First, his fellow servants are distressed and angered by what has happened, sufficiently so to report it to the king; and the king, in rage, summons him and spells out to him why his pardon is about to be revoked. For a far greater wrong than the man's debts is his refusal to enact to another the same mercy he has himself received. Therefore he will pay his own full penalty . . .

Structurally, therefore, the story begins from and ends with the king's judgement. Within that judgement absolute mercy is available and is applied: but it cannot be sustained where its reality is denied, as a gift which having been received, must be shared. The various 'chapters' of the story depend on the development of this truth.

Metonymy and metaphor

There are certain metonymic details it is worth clarifying. The scale of the first debt, while no doubt owing something to a touch of deliberate storytelling exaggeration, is in fact revealing since it gives us the real nature of the setting. This is the court of a considerable king, calling before him the local governors of the provinces to give account of their provinces' tributes. (Such governors could be, in fact often were, still slaves.) So the huge debt would be the tax tribute owing over several years from a particular province. We should remember that a talent, the highest currency unit, was the equivalent of fifteen years' wages for a hired labourer. 'Ten thousand' was the largest sum in reckoning. So if this local governor had been keeping all the tax to himself during this period, he had lived lavishly indeed.

The denarius, by contrast, was the equivalent of one day's wages for a labourer. This debt therefore does not suggest any maladministration of taxes, but more probably a loan, made out of the very profit the first man had illicitly gained.

The threatened punishment could only be applied (under Jewish law) if it was a case of theft, and the thief could not restore what he had taken. It is possible to argue that this implies the court was Gentile, but given the probable cause of the debt, that does not seem necessary. (An Israelite could not be sold unless it was a case of theft and restitution could not be made.) But while this first punishment threatened is realistic, the last is rather less so: torture was part of the stock-in-trade of the traditional storyteller, rather than practised in Jewish prisons. (Though for all the legal proscription of it, Herod the Great is reported to have had no compunction in its use. And the details of Christ's treatment in Roman hands suggest that 'torture' was no unfamiliar concept to Jesus' listeners.)

So much for the metonymic detail. What of the metaphoric mode? It is introduced, as we have seen, by Jesus' deliberate linking of the issue of 'forgiveness' in his discussion with Peter, with the very nature of the 'kingdom of heaven', that is, God's domain. Magnanimity beyond conceiving – forgiveness 'up to seventy times seven', i.e., without limit – is the law of heaven: and *'for this reason'* the kingdom of heaven is like a king ... This is reinforced by Jesus' comment as the story ends with the torturers: 'So my heavenly Father will also do to everyone of you, if you do not forgive your brother or sister from your heart.'

The immediate meaning of this to Jesus' listeners – in this case, it would seem likely, the disciples themselves – would have personal application to *them*: 'forgiveness' must be exercised not by prescription or rote but as a habit of the heart. But beyond this we find in this parable perhaps the most complete – and dire – summary of the message Jesus had so pressed upon his listeners in his teaching, his stories and his actions: that 'being righteous before God' through the grace of God, invoked through sin-offerings and the like, could not be limited to one group who took it to themselves and then refused its application to others. The religious leaders stand indicted, because they owed the debts of the whole nation for which they were responsible to God; and God would forgive them. But claiming that forgiveness for themselves, they then refused it to 'the outsiders' and instead consigned them to the very darkness they had just been freed from. *This* was the unforgivable sin in Jesus' eyes: their inability to take that forgiveness into their hearts as an active dynamic, but rather to see it as a mechanistic action which had worked for them but which it was not their responsibility to make work for others. Perhaps the most terrible instance of this is in their reply to Judas's grief-stricken cry of guilt after the Crucifixion, of 'I have sinned by betraying righteous blood': 'What is that to us? See to it yourself,' they say (Matt. 27:3–4).

So the Judgement of Judgement Day, which always contained within it the reality of Mercy, would be foreclosed, because they had not entered into it: they were not 'clothed' with it, as a wedding garment; they did not speak its language, and hence were 'dumb'. Hence the language of the End-Time at the end of the parable.

The story for today?

This is the darkest parable in the Bible, because it is like a development into un-redemption of the 'Elder Brother' part of the parable of the Prodigal Son. It suggests, in our endless search through human history for the way in which justice and mercy can properly be balanced, the limits of divine forgiveness. They are limits which, terrifyingly, we as humanity *choose to impose for ourselves*. So the story addresses us as we ponder on the divine encounter which is the experience of all, in some form, would we but recognise it. That encounter in which we have to face the ultimate reality of things, this story suggests, is full of potential for forgiveness of all that mars our lives, and freedom from the burden of it. But if we do not make that forgiveness and freedom so wholly our own that we live by it in relation to others, then we foreclose its reality for ourselves. For mercy is a dynamic, and to receive it we have to become channels through which it flows, irrigating and bringing new life indeed in our own hearts and lives, but flowing strongly *beyond* them to all those whose lives we touch. It is the dynamic which flows through 'Thou shalt love the Lord thy God, and thy neighbour as thyself'. Indeed, it is the power which makes that commandment effective. For 'forgiving' is the work of obedient faith, its response to the grace of God, which is why the disciples, recognising the magnitude of the heart-change needed, cry out 'Lord, increase our faith!'

And that is why the story of its rejection is dreadful: of a piece with the Passion. It is where the Cross and the parables meet; and that is the darkest place on earth.

'The Rich Man and Lazarus the Beggar' (Luke 16:19–31)

The story of 'The Rich Man and the Beggar' appears only in Luke, where it is embedded in a sequence of teaching which follows Jesus' telling of the parables of 'The Prodigal Son' and 'The Untrustworthy Manager'. Perhaps the key to that whole

sequence of teaching, which extends after the parable of 'The
Rich Man and Lazarus the Beggar' into the next chapter, ending
with the story of 'The Servant's Reward', is to be found in
Christ's comment recorded in Luke 16:16:

> *'The law and the prophets were in effect till John came; since*
> *then the good news of the kingdom of God is proclaimed, and*
> *everyone is strongly urged to enter it. But it is easier for heaven*
> *and earth to pass away, than for one stroke of a letter in the law*
> *to be dropped.'*

For this sets out very clearly the confrontation which is at
the heart of Jesus' teaching: the absolute nature of God's justice,
as expressed in the law, and as it secures the ultimate 'setting
right' of all wrong with the victory of 'righteousness', goodness;
and, balancing this, the absolute nature of God's mercy, which
covers not only the penitent sinner but the one who would be
penitent, could he but see how. The language of 'the kingdom
of heaven', necessarily redressing an imbalance, has emphasised the loving mercy of God, the freedom available under his
rule. But that mercy and freedom are not at the *expense* of the
absoluteness of right, but a *part of it*. Hence, any assumption
that this is a libertine's charter is dangerously wrong. For the
laws by which 'heaven and earth' both operate are those of
the righteous God, in whom justice and mercy, righteousness
and peace are equal in one larger law.

The parable of 'The Rich Man and Lazarus the Beggar' relates
to the absoluteness of this ultimate law. Its initial material is
the stuff of traditional storytelling: a rich man and a beggar
are the nicely contrasted polar opposites of a number of possible
story developments, from the magical to the realistic. Nevertheless, while there is therefore a metonymy, a coherent world, of
storytelling, there is equally a metonymy of everyday life. For
all Jesus' hearers would 'know' Lazarus: that is, have seen him
and his kind at their regular begging pitches daily. And all knew
the big houses of rich men, and the sumptuous extravagance of
their life-style. The two characters are brought together simply
because this beggar has his pitch outside the door of the rich
man's house. (He is, incidentally, the only character in all the
parables to be given a name, one which means 'God helps'.
How he comes by it, and whether it is by association with one

who *did* 'come back from the dead' (John 11:43, 44), it is impossible to tell. 'Dives', the name given sometimes to the rich man, is simply the Latin word for 'rich'.)

The metonymic detail of the rich man is delightful. He is dressed in 'purple and fine linen' – colour and texture of aristocracy – and he 'feasted sumptuously' every day. Remembering that banquets were public, open to outsiders to come and stand round the edges and gather such fragments as they could, Lazarus would be able to see this feasting and those attending. But he is a cripple (he 'lay' at the gate) and (like Job whose state he resembles) he suffers from a skin disease. So he is not able to come in and gather those fragments from the table (which would not so much be crumbs, as the bread used to dip the sauces, or to wipe the fingers clean). The dogs lick his sores: it is not clear whether this is a final indignity; almost certainly it would seem so.

Thus far the metonymy of 'this' world. When he and the rich man die and are found in the 'next' world, the metonymy is of traditional popular Jewish belief, which Jesus uses as a vehicle without making any comment on it. Now the positions are reversed. While nothing is said of Lazarus' funeral, he is, as is traditional with blessed souls worldwide and down through the ages, 'carried away by the angels'. The rich man, by comparison, has a funeral – 'was buried' – and is then discovered in Hades, being tormented. Lazarus is in the highest place of honour in heaven, 'by the side of Abraham'. The topography of traditional other-world metonymy is spelt out to us: the chasm between heaven and Hades ('a great gulf fixed') which is impassable; the agonizing flames of hell. Against this traditional background the dialogue takes place.

It becomes clear that the whole story is simply the vehicle for this dialogue. Its first element is a plea by the rich man for relief: just one drop of water from heaven will ease his torment: can Lazarus be sent with such a drop on the tip of his finger to cool the rich man's tongue? It is worth noticing that the rich man still has that arrogance which sees Lazarus as in servile role – 'being sent' to minister to him. Abraham's reply is factual rather than unkind, addressing the rich man as 'child'. There is surprisingly little blame in what he says: indeed, their relative positions could be seen as simply the reversal of fortunes, with no moral judgement involved; the rich man had things good in his earthly life, and Lazarus suffered: so now there must be reverse.

But clearly more is implied than this, for the rich man now becomes urgent that his five brothers, still alive, should be warned. Can Lazarus be sent to them?

But what is it that they should be warned of, if no moral wrongdoing is involved? Clearly implicit, therefore, in the story is that something in the life-style of the rich man has *deserved* this punishment, something, warned of which, his brothers could avoid. Abraham's reply is significant: 'They have Moses and the prophets, they should listen to them.' The rich man is urgent: 'But if someone goes from the dead . . .' The climax is in Abraham's response, the point for which the story has been told: 'If they do not listen to Moses and the prophets, neither will they be convinced even if someone rises from the dead.'

How may we understand Jesus' point here for his listeners? One clue to the metaphoric mode which unlocks the story lies in the fact that his society would view the beggar as a sinner *because* of his misfortunes: they are an indication he has deserved God's chastisement. So that for him to be haled to heaven is not the development in the story which would be expected. It precisely reverses the valuation society has put on the two men: the rich man 'good' because he has been blessed with the good things of life, the poor man 'sinful' because of his disasters. It becomes clear how the theme of Job is running through the story. In the event, it challenges the facile assumptions concerning 'righteousness' and 'sin', suggesting they are less a matter of external measure than has been assumed. Lazarus is the equivalent of 'my servant Job', whose sufferings are a matter of a test of faithfulness, not of sin.

Is *this* the point of the dialogue? Hardly: its force emerges before any dialogue occurs. So we have a double thrust in this parable, one element making the same point as Job, the other concerned with the issue of how people may understand the absoluteness, in the light of eternity, of God's law of 'setting right', which the self-indulgent rich man has failed to do. What the dialogue pinpoints is that if a nation cannot hear the wisdom it has already been given – the inestimable divine gift of the Law, and the prophets who challenged people to observe it – which addresses amongst other things the inequity between rich and poor, then nothing, no intervention from beyond the grave, will draw them to repentance and obedience. This is the force of Jesus' message to his immediate listeners – crowd, religious leaders, disciples.

Given the raising of Lazarus and the Resurrection of Christ (though we do not know whether Luke knew of the raising of Lazarus) the reference to 'someone rising from the dead' must inevitably have taken on a particular meaning for the young Church. For Jesus' original listeners the story would both insist on the inclusion of the 'outsider', the beggar, the supposed sinner, in the Kingdom of heaven; and warn that the truth had been given them long ago by Moses, *so they could not plead ignorance.* For the young Christian community it would be a story which ran with their own experience, of the disbelief of those to whom they told the good news that 'Christ was risen'. What had been foreseen by the prophets was no more convincing to their mocking contemporaries 'even if someone rises from the dead'. So for them the stress on the absolute unshakeability of God's word, through Moses and the prophets, confirmed in the death and rising of Jesus, would be of profound comfort. 'Not one stroke of the law would be dropped', for Jesus was the enactment of that law in the life of the nation.

The story today

Although this is a richly fascinating story, it is also a darkly depressing one. It finds its place here, in this chapter of parables of disobedience, because it is about the springs of that disobedience: *the refusal to hear.*

For Christian history is bound up with this 'refusal to hear'. In the long contention between agnostic reason and unproven revelation the nature of the issue as one of life and death is rarely brought to the surface. This parable faces that truth. It suggests that life is lived within certain realities which have been spelt out for humanity in a variety of ways (cf. Rom. 1:18–23). We can live our life as though these realities are in no way relevant, or as though they have no substance. But there will be a time of divine encounter – death is a good image of this – when the hard, concrete nature of these realities is experienced as formative of existence itself. Would we not wish, should we pass through that experience, to send warnings back to those we care about, that this is so? Yet that may not be; and is not only not necessary, but not effective, the parable urges.

For all the material for discerning these realities is already available in this life. The trouble is not lack of guidance (through both reason and revelation) but a refusal to accept that guidance. A usurpation of the listening heart takes place, and it becomes dominated by purple and fine linen, by indulgence or self-seeking or the will to power. The five brothers of the story are doomed if of their own volition they will not turn to the way of justice and mercy spelt out by Moses and the prophets. And for those who have encountered the Teller of this tale, both when it was told and so right down the centuries, they too must attend to the realities it points to, before it is too late.

Section Three

The Last Things

12 The Parables of 'The Wheat and the Weeds', 'The Dragnet' and 'The Closed Door'

WE HAVE A CURIOUS relationship with the concept of the 'Last Things' in our contemporary culture. On the one hand we are fascinated, appalled and attracted by the notion of 'apocalypse'. A society which has lived through the twentieth century, which has become intensely globally aware, and which has the technological capacity to self-destruct, could hardly be other than aware of the potential of apocalypse. So films, drama and novels explore it, sometimes facilely, occasionally with depth. On the other hand, the kind of thinking which lies behind biblical apocalyptic language is almost wholly alien to us. For the Bible's apocalypse is not random, nor ultimately human-determined – though humanity may provide some of its mechanisms. Rather it is part of the coming Judgement of God, the Day, the terrible Day of Wrath, when time and the designs of God come to their fruition. In that sense, though it is full of terror in biblical presentation, it is also full of *hope*: because it marks the beginning of that 'setting right', that 'sorting out' which will remove all that clogs goodness ('all causes of sin' Matt. 13:41b) so that the 'righteous' will 'shine like the sun in the kingdom of their Father' (Matt. 13:43). It is, in other words, about the establishment of Justice – uncompromised, uncorrupt and large enough for all – as our home. Because it is large enough for all – at least, the Judgement Jesus speaks of has this astonishing capacity – its obverse is Mercy.

Many of the parables we have already read are given 'edge' and 'bite' by the context Jesus implies of a critical, and imminent, encounter with God: which in his world would be understood and presented in terms of the 'Day of Judgement', the 'End-Time', the 'Last Things'. Our own world has difficulty with this, and not only because of the particular structure of religious thought which lies behind it. There is also for many of us the problem that an open-ended universe – physical, historical, moral, spiritual – is the category within which we think. So while the notion that 'time must have a stop' is not beyond our acceptance, since we are conscious of some of the finitudes of our earth and indeed our universe; yet the sense of this as 'the consummation of all things' – of all the other universes we are slowly becoming aware of and guessing at, almost beyond our conceiving – this goes hard with the contemporary mind.

Yet I think it need not, for the Bible's concern is with earth and its human inhabitants and their relationship with their Creator. It does indeed reflect the majesty and inscrutability of the earth's own universe and suggests catastrophe among the stars – consistently: compare Isaiah 34:4, 'All the host of heaven shall rot away, and the skies roll up like a scroll', with 2 Peter 3:10, 12:

> But the day of the Lord will come like a thief, and then the heavens will pass away with a loud noise, and the elements will be dissolved with fire, and the earth and everything that is done on it will be burned up . . . the coming of the day of God, because of which the heavens will be set ablaze and dissolved, and the elements will melt with fire.

But this catastrophe is in *our* universe – no others are hinted at and even so it is but the prelude to a new 'creation': 'But, in accordance with his promise, we wait for new heavens and a new earth, *where righteousness is at home*' (2 Pet. 3:13).

As we approach this last group of parables, therefore, whose purpose is specifically related to the End-Time, we need to enter sympathetically into what is being glimpsed through both the metonymic and metaphoric modes of the stories. For something is being explored here which is too overwhelming, too intensely dazzling, for direct gaze, so that only through the guarded lens of parable can we begin to discern its outline. That 'something' is to do with the consummation of our human relationship with God, and the place in it at which 'Justice' and 'Mercy' reach their ultimate point of balance.

The five parables we shall read in these two chapters – one of them. 'The Dragnet', is really a micro-parable, an appendage to the story of 'The Wheat and the Weeds' – these five parables explore some of the fundamentals of this 'ultimate point'. There is the question of who will be enlarged by it, and who will not, and *why*; and what will happen to those who are not. There is the question of whether there really *is* an 'ultimate point', and what its nature is. How absolute, how final, are its dispositions?

Finally there is the nature of the expectation, of what being caught up into that ultimate balance of Justice and Mercy – for ever – may mean in terms of quality of life.

If we read these five parables carefully, we get some hints, some piercing glimpse, indeed, of the indescribable reality which exists behind the images Jesus presents, through the religious language of his people's experience of God. Those glimpses address our own preoccupations and anxieties with surprising contemporaneity. So to these last stories we must now turn.

'The Wheat and the Weeds' and 'The Dragnet' (Matt. 13:24–30 and 36b–43; Matt. 13:47–50)

These two parables, which appear only in Matthew, are rounded off by closely similar comments: 'The Son of Man will send his angels, and they will collect out of his kingdom all causes of sin and all evildoers, and they will throw them into the furnace of fire, where there will be weeping and gnashing of teeth' (Matt. 13:41, 42, concluding the allegorical interpretation of 'The Wheat and the Weeds'); 'The angels will come and separate the evil from the righteous and throw them into the furnace of fire, where there will be weeping and gnashing of teeth' (Matt. 13:49, 50, concluding the parable of 'The Dragnet'). So the two are perceived as directly related, and the relation is apocalyptic. They are embedded in a section of teaching which begins with the parable of 'The Sower' and its allegorical interpretation and continues with 'The Mustard Seed' and 'The Yeast'; and, after the parable of 'The Wheat and the Weeds' continues with 'The Treasure' and 'The Pearl' before the little parable of 'The Dragnet' concludes the section. It is worth noticing that Jesus is described as teaching through the medium of these stories first beside the lake, and then from a boat upon it while the 'great crowd' stood on the shore. So this provides a naturalistic setting for the metonymic detail of 'The Sower', 'The Mustard Seed', 'The Wheat and the

Weeds' – the landscape of which would be catching his eye as
he spoke – and 'The Dragnet', which could indeed have been
in operation further along the shore.

In one sense 'The Wheat and the Weeds' continues the theme
of 'The Sower', as well as its setting. For in 'The Sower' Jesus
is exploring the mystery of how some 'hear' the 'word of
the kingdom', while others do not. But it is the mystery of the
process of being 'rooted' in the grace of the Kingdom which is
under scrutiny in that story. In 'The Wheat and the Weeds' we
move on, to a related problem. How is it that a 'just' God
allows the wicked to flourish alongside the 'good', apparently
undiscerned in the scales of justice in human life? It is a question
as alive today as at the time of the tale. As we shall see, however,
the metaphoric mode of the parable adjusts the question and
its dimensions. To appreciate that, we need first to look at the
metonymic detail which creates the world of the story.

The metonymy of *'The Wheat and the Weeds'*
It is a familiar world to Christ's listeners, instantly recognisable
until we come to the question of 'the enemy' who did this. The
problem of weeds amongst grain was (and is) the perennial one
for farmers: the local weed, the darnel, would be of particular
nuisance value because in early stages of growth its young
shoots and that of the corn or wheat were virtually indis-
tinguishable. So if attacked too early the good shoots could
easily be uprooted as well as the noxious. When a little more
fully grown, and easily distinguishable, the sturdiness of the
darnel root and its spread meant that again good grain could
be easily damaged in sifting out the weeds. Sometimes farmers
opted for this so that their crop should have maximum space
and soil. But an alternative – in this case the chosen one – was
to let weeds and wheat grow together till harvest time, when
the two could very easily be separated: then the weeds could
be bound together in great bundles, leaving the wheat unsullied
ready for reaping. The virtue of this was that the good grain
would not be damaged, since it was to be uprooted anyway.
And there was always extra labour at harvest time to share the
burden of this sorting of weed from grain. It was, however,
vital that at this late point the sifting of the one from the other
was effective and completely thorough: for the *seeds of the darnel
were poisonous*, a fact with significance in the *metaphoric* mode.

So much for the basic story, one which would draw nods from the entire crowd, many of whom would be the day-labourers of a dozen harvest times whose hands had been blistered doing precisely this job.

The story as metaphor
What of the metaphoric mode? Leaving aside the complication of the 'enemy' who sowed the weeds – which is certainly a bridge into a metaphoric mode – we may pick up the meta-phoric dimension through the beginning of the story: the Kingdom of heaven 'may be compared to someone who sowed good seed'. This is a good farmer, looking towards a fruitful harvest, and taking appropriate steps to achieve it: it is not cheap but 'good' seed that is sown. Yet weeds come up along-side the young blades of wheat. So we are presented with the greatest mystery of a domain that is God's: the preparation is good, yet there are weeds – yet, that is, there is evil. Evil which, if not eventually checked, has poisonous consequences. We are instantly face to face with the huge and inscrutable mystery of evil in a God-ruled world, that mystery which so anguishes us still. The interpolation of 'the enemy' offers an explanation to which I shall return in a moment, one in the language of Jesus' times. But leaving it aside, we have a story which does not attempt to explain our interim experience of this terrible mystery, but which does speak very powerfully of its *resolution* in due time. In other words, the main thrust, through its meta-phoric mode, of the basic story, is not about 'why' evil, but of what the *end* of evil may confidently be expected to be.

We are back to the 'law of increase and fruitfulness' we looked at earlier in our readings. This is a primary law in God's domain. Therefore just as the farmer will allow certain things to develop in his field in a carefully balanced judgement as to what is in his intended crop's most fruitful interest, so will God. The implication is that the 'evildoers' and the 'causes of sin' which the allegorical interpretation (Matt. 13:41) refers to, are not divinely unobserved, and will not be allowed to destroy the 'good grain', i.e., the marvellous crop of salvation and righteousness which will be the 'harvest home' of ultimate time. What is evil in human life will in due course be dealt with, but not in such a way as to put at risk the coming to full fruitfulness of humanity as humanity was meant to be, placed on earth to be. So the story affirms on the one hand the ultimate sovereignty of God, and on the other the *unperceived* care with which the needs of 'righteous' humanity are assessed and protected, so that it may come to full harvest.

The 'complication' in the story

And what of 'the enemy?' Metonymically this is a complication, a detail, that would indeed be possible in the world of Jesus' first listeners, since feuds, between individual farmers or between villages, would inevitably give rise from time to time to the sort of 'dirty tricks' that range from burning crops (cf. Judg. 15:4–6) to in some way spoiling them. But, while this no doubt did happen, it is much less a matter of everyday life than is the basic story, and much more the sort of development that belongs in another metonymy, that of the traditional storyteller. If we move into *this* metonymic world we are then in a rather different parable: that of two farmers feuding, one of whom has excellent seed to plant and the other of whom is determined to prevent his rival's excellence. The second succeeds in sowing weeds 'while everybody was asleep' (13:25), to the extent that it causes comment. These are not the incidental weeds every farmer knows, but so widespread and strong that their cause is not natural, but effected through malice.

How will the farmer deal with it? Not by rushing in and uprooting the offending plants, to the detriment of his own crop (as his enemy and rival may hope), but by waiting patiently till his own – excellent – crop has reached its full strength and fruitfulness; and *then* eradicating by its very roots the handiwork of his enemy.

While the story, with this complication, has much the same ending – so that it could be called the parable of 'The Triumphant Crop' – yet the emphasis now falls on the struggle between the farmer and 'an enemy'.

So in metaphoric mode, what we have here is a parallel to the story of the serpent in Eden in the Book of Genesis, moving on to a kind of miniature apocalypse at the end of the parable, with the harvest being the 'salvation' harvest which has survived the work of 'the Enemy', and the weeds being 'all causes of sin and all evildoers', which end in the 'furnace of fire' when gathered in by 'angels'. Thus Jesus' first listeners would hear it, if the complication of the plot was originally there and not either an addition or a fusion of two stories. The early Church would hear it thus also. But they would also hear it as a message counselling patience: the process of salvation is in the hands of God, and therefore premature attempts to stamp out the evil amongst which the Church lives are futile.

Moreover, if the parable is applied – as it may well have been – directly to the community of faith, then the implication is that there should be no attempt to make ultimate judgements about fellow members' 'righteousness'. For the time of such revealing is not yet. This is a warning which runs through Jesus' own teaching and appears later in Paul's letters. 'Do not judge, that you may not be judged. For with the judgment you make you will be judged' (Matt. 7:1, 2a): i.e., you are not skilled to distinguish the darnel of evil from the wheat of righteousness; it is too early, and you may wreak destruction in attempting it. What is implied here, of course, is that the 'self-righteousness' and 'complacency' which so often attend the attempt to judge others destroys the very goodness which the attempt to root out evil has been meant to protect. Hence Christ's attacks on the self-righteousness of the religious leaders. Thus, also, Paul, to the Roman Christians: 'Why do you pass judgment on your brother or sister? . . . For we will all stand before the judgment seat of God . . .' (Rom. 14:10). And again, 'Therefore do not pronounce judgment before the time, before the Lord comes, who will bring to light the things now hidden in darkness and will disclose the purposes of the heart' (1 Cor. 4:5).

The parable of 'The Dragnet'

This is a miniature version of the basic pattern (without 'the enemy') of the parable of 'The Wheat and the Weeds'. Metonymi-cally again the detail is recognisable and realistic. Such huge nets were regularly used either fastened between two boats, or dropped from one boat and then hauled in by the attached strong ropes to the shore. Their mesh was such that everything was caught in them – all sorts of aquatic life, edible and non-edible. Some fish was ruled as 'unclean' (see Lev. 11:10f) and not to be eaten – fish without fins or scales, for instance. So once the net was ashore all these would have to be sifted out

from 'the good' which would be put in baskets for carrying to
the market.

The metaphoric mode takes us into precisely the same spiritual pattern as the earlier parable. These creatures swarm side
by side, unseparated, until a moment of reckoning; and then
they are distinguished. Even thus it is with 'God's domain',
swarming with life that is 'good' and 'bad': the day will come
when distinctions will finally be made determining all future
existence.

The day will come ...

This takes us from issues about the prolonged period in which
divine Justice is not discernibly active, to the insistence, in these
parables, and in those we are about to read, on the certainty of
a future moment when this Justice will be discerned by all,
overwhelmingly enacted. All things are perceived, in the
context of such a certainty, to come to consummation. After
that point all will be changed, utterly changed, and there will
be no going back.

The absoluteness of this encounter with divine Justice is
matched by the absoluteness of its consequence: a separating
out. 'Sifting out' means that what is not yet purified must go,
and what refuses purification, rejects the need for it or is
resistant to it, finds itself separated from that which would be
pure, lest it 'poison' it. What this might mean, in the language
of Jesus' day and in our own, is the material of the next parables.

'The Closed Door' (Luke 13:24–30)

This parable appears only in Luke, and is placed in the context
of Jesus' journey to Jerusalem. He is moving through towns
and villages, teaching as he goes; but always inexorably moving
towards what he knows will be his own decisive encounter. He
tells this story in response to a question from someone in the
crowd: 'Lord, will only a few be saved?' (13:23).

What is the *content* of that question? It clearly must have
arisen from the teaching he was giving, and therefore would
certainly relate at one level to the imminent critical engagement
with God which Jesus was declaring, and which would be
understood by many to be the judgement of God, possibly the

final Judgement. But it has wider and deeper content than the specific catastrophe which did indeed come, the destruction of Jerusalem. We may gather much of that fuller meaning from the parable itself.

The core of the parable of 'The Closed Door' is introduced by the image of the 'narrow door', to which we find a parallel in Matthew 7:13–14: 'Enter through the narrow gate; for the gate is wide and the road easy that leads to destruction, and there are many who take it. For the gate is narrow and the road hard that leads to life, and there are few who find it.'

This *concept* is the same as in the beginning of the parable in Luke: 'Strive to enter through the narrow door; for many, I tell you, will try to enter and will not be able' (13:24): we begin, that is, with the observation that the 'way to life' is not easily entered upon. But there are quite significant differences, both in the images and in what lies behind them. The Matthew image is of a journey, with alternative routes, the vital one being the narrowest and hardest to find. The Lucan picture is of the door to a dwelling house; and the problem is not in finding it, but in gaining admittance through it. So while the primary point, that of 'difficulty', is consistent, the images take us in different ways in developing the truths about that 'difficulty'.

And this leads us to the core of the story.

The story

At the heart of the story is a scene not unlike that of the parable of 'Importunity at Midnight'. It is a village (or city) street scene, and it is night, for the owner has 'got up and shut the door' (Luke 13:25a), dropping the great bar across for security, just as in the earlier parable. He has a house full of guests, friends and intimates, who have arrived before 'locking up' time. The ending of the parable suggests, sketched in by implication as background to the parable, a gathering at the house for celebration, a banquet or feast. 'Then people will come . . . and will eat in the kingdom of God' (13:29).

But now, after the door is shut, another group arrives – late. They request admission, as they 'begin to stand outside and to knock at the door, saying "Lord, open to us"' (13:25b). The householder's reply is the response of any sensible man to an unknown crowd knocking on his door in the middle of the night: 'I do not know where you come from' (13.25c). They instantly claim an intimacy of relationship ('We ate and drank with you and you taught in our streets') which he dismisses as spurious. As well it could be, for this could have been a distant and passive relationship: the 'eating' and 'drinking' could well be envisaged as their being in the same banqueting hall as himself – but far removed from him. And the fact that he 'taught in their streets' gave them no claim of relationship *unless they had responded to his teaching*. (We noticed in an earlier chapter that simply moving about in a curious crowd around Jesus did not constitute 'following' him.) So we need not be surprised at his reiterated response: 'I do not know where you come from; go away from me'.

Thus far the metonymy of the parable is unbrokenly realistic, completely recognisable. Even when the owner of the house adds to his adjuration to them to 'go away' the epithet, 'all you evildoers!', there is realism. For if he did *not* know them, if they were merely a mob who had heard there was a party and were trying to gate-crash it – which is broadly the picture being suggested – then 'evildoers' might indeed be a realistic description of them.

But at this point the metaphoric mode breaks through insistently. For one thing, the house owner is described by these latecomers as one who 'taught in their streets'. So he is not only a householder gathering in the chosen for a banquet, he is a 'teacher' – a prophet. And so he takes on the persona of one who speaks the word of God; and the way is prepared not only for the term 'evildoer' – to which we shall return – but to the comments which complete and summarise the parable's meaning. First among these is: 'There will be weeping and gnashing of teeth' (a phrase used primarily by Matthew and apocalyptic in reference) 'when you see Abraham and Isaac and Jacob and all the prophets in the kingdom of God, and you yourselves thrown out.'

This clearly for Jesus' listeners – and for the early Church reading the story 'collected' in this way – makes the story one concerning the End-Time. Luke as editor may have 'placed' this statement immediately after the parable, as a piece of Jesus' teaching which neatly summarised its point. Or it may have been in the original story, though the change in style, from narrative to exhortatory, suggests not. In any case what it emphasises is that inherent in the parable is a picture of those in true and profound relationship with God (such as Abraham, Isaac and Jacob and the prophets exemplify), at home with him in security. And spurious claimants such as 'you yourselves' are 'thrown out'. Who are the 'yourselves' of this comment? Clearly, some who regard themselves as having an intimacy with the Lord God which he in fact denies. Those religious leaders whom Jesus so often castigated must come into this category, but it need not be so narrow. Since the question about whether 'only a few' would be saved had come from someone in the crowd, it seems more probable, particularly given the reference to teaching 'in our streets', that Jesus is addressing the nation as a whole, indicating that neither race nor proximity are sufficient for 'salvation'.

The second interpretative comment confirms this: 'Then people will come from east and west, from north and south, and will eat in the kingdom of God.' This has a parallel in Matthew 8:11, 12 which explicitly draws out the 'national' implication: 'I tell you, many will come from east and west and eat with Abraham and Isaac and Jacob in the kingdom, while the heirs of the kingdom will be thrown into outer darkness, where there will be weeping and gnashing of teeth.' The 'you yourselves' who are 'thrown out' are here 'the heirs of the kingdom'. To this, Luke adds a third interpretative comment, found embedded elsewhere in Jesus' teaching in both Mark (10:31) and – twice – in Matthew, in variant forms (19:30 and 20:16): 'Indeed, some are last who will be first, and some are first who will be last.' So for Luke the story is addressed to the nation, and is strongly supportive of the claims of the Gentiles, non-Jews 'from east and west, from north and south', who, though thought of as 'last' in access to God's domain, will, it is implied, gather for the banquet of heaven ahead of those who had been 'first', the 'heirs of the kingdom'.

Crossover language

But there is much more to the crossover language of metonymy and metaphor in this parable than its fairly immediately obvious application to a complacent nation and its self-righteous leaders. For here we must return to that command, 'Go away from me, all you evildoers!' This is a point where metonymy and metaphor meet, for this is a direct quotation from the Psalms, and familiar therefore to all faithful worshipping Jews, part of the metonymy of their religious culture. It comes from Psalm 6, a psalm of lament and grief at the psalmist's sense of being misjudged by his enemies, combined with a yearning that God should vindicate him rather than in his wrath 'discipline' him; for he is 'languishing'. The verse quoted (verse 8), marks the triumphant turning point of the psalm, from anxiety, distress and diffidence to confidence in the vindication of God:

> Depart from me, all you workers of evil,
> for the Lord has heard the sound of my weeping.
> The Lord has heard my supplication;
> the Lord accepts my prayer.
> All my enemies shall be ashamed and
> struck with terror;
> They shall turn back, and in a moment be put to shame.

How does this help us enter more profoundly into the meaning of the parable? If the note of 'vindication' is being picked up, then this must mean that those who are the 'evildoers' are the ones who have added to the suffering of the speaker who has suffered 'grief', and waste 'because of all [his] foes'. They have caused grief and been identified as 'evildoers' because of their *profound misjudgement of God's servant*. Who then are those safely within, who have come from 'the north and the south, the east and the west'? A teaching passage in Matthew, parallel to this parable in Luke, offers us a reading:

> *'Not everyone who says to me "Lord, Lord", will enter the kingdom of heaven, but only the one who does the will of my Father in heaven. On that day many will say to me, "Lord, Lord, did we not prophesy in your name, and cast out demons in your name, and do many deeds of power in your name?" Then I will declare to them, "I never knew you; go away from me, you evildoers." '* (Matt. 7:21–23)

'Only one who does the will of my Father in heaven.' We have returned to the law of active commitment and obedience. And now we are in a position to make a fuller reading of the parable.

A reading

For those who are 'shut out' are defined in two ways. They are 'late': the door is already closed. And they are not, whatever their claims, known to the owner of the house. From the biblical material we have observed as a kind of 'backing' lying behind the story, it is clear that 'being known' to 'the owner of the house' is to be in the kind of intimate relationship with him that grows from a wise judgement of who and what he is – what the significance of his 'teaching', for instance (unlike the 'enemies' of the Psalmist); a relationship which is fostered and developed by the *practice* of that wise judgement in the lives of those who have made it ('doing the will of my Father in heaven'). It is those who facilely do not recognise the Messenger of God, but despise and mistreat him; or at best cynically mis-represent him, and so lose the dynamic of the word of God in the way they should live: *these* are the 'evildoers' who, not known, are 'thrown out' from the party.

And the 'lateness'? Continually in these parables we see an insistence that in the nature of things a resolution must and will one day be made. Time, extended time, generous extra time, is given; but the fact that God is patient does not mean he will never act: it means that he is more patient with way-wardness than humanly we can conceive. But at some point in the *divine* history of things they will move to their consum-mation, the owner will 'get up and shut the door', and after that, by definition, all comers are 'unknown' and so 'excluded'. This resonates with the continual warning of the prophets through Jewish history, that the moment of final decision will indeed come.

A parable for today?

We can turn now to that question with which we began: what is the *content* of the query, 'Lord, will only a few be saved?' What does 'saved' mean for us as we read this story in a culture and mindset remote indeed from the language and religious thought patterns which colour it?

The story helps us. For 'salvation' is not described in the story other than by implication through two details. First of all, it is the experience of 'inclusion' as opposed to 'exclusion'; and that 'inclusion' is glossed for us a little. It is 'inclusion' in the continuum that starts with the story of the inherent relationship between God and his creation, and which is typified, through 'Abraham, Isaac and Jacob', by a personal 'family' bond between God and the human race. To be 'included' in God's eternal domain, in 'the kingdom of heaven' therefore, is to realise, and be taken up into, that continuum of loving relationship with a Creator God which gives humanity its profoundest 'rootedness'. To be 'included' is to be rescued from rootlessness and know and affirm where one belongs and in what relationship; following that up through a way of living – 'doing the will' – which is the proper life-style of the one who belongs. The parable's extra force, for us as for the early Church, is that it is the Teller of the tale who himself effects the 'rescue from unbelonging'.

Salvation, therefore, is to belong where one truly belongs, to recognise it in time, and so to affirm it in the heart that it issues in a habit of mind and body proper to where one belongs, and to whom one belongs. It is to this that Christ invites, it is *in* this that Christ enables.

But salvation is therefore also 'celebration', for the image of the 'eating together' in the Kingdom is a festive one. That is: who one properly is, and to whom one belongs as a human being in God's creation, is a cause for great delight and rejoicing, for celebration. Most of all this is so when all that would deflect one from this recognition of where one belongs has finally been left behind, shut out by the power of God's merciful Judgement, and so a torment no more.

It follows that 'exclusion' is a state of permanent rootlessness, a refusal to recognise affinity, or a continual temporising such that one becomes steadily less able to take the decisive step of aligning oneself with the continuum of God's creation.

Hence the emphasis on the possibility of being 'too late'. If we reflect briefly again on that image of the 'narrow gate', we can transfer it to our own language of a 'window of opportunity'. We are accustomed to the language of 'space shuttles' which must catch that 'window of opportunity' or matters will not be favourably aligned again, for months, years, perhaps for ever. To be 'late' in the terms of this parable is to have missed the 'window of opportunity' with God. For a part of the 'way things are' is that relationships can be evaded and evaded for just so long, and then, as we know in human terms, the moment for it is past. And if we remember the perpetual dynamic of

God's 'law of increase' as we read of it earlier in parables, we recognise how these things connect. Nothing remains unchanged indefinitely. A point of progression is reached beyond which something has changed and become something else, in the spiritual as in the material world. Once that point has been reached it is not possible to return. The Owner has 'got up and shut the door'. The long, long 'time' (to be thought of as not only 'temporal', but spiritually 'spatial') given for emerging from temporising – 'eating and drinking' with God, but only at a distance; seeing him 'teaching in our streets', but not engaging with him – all that lengthy time of possibility must come to an end, when the 'possibility' either ceases to be, or is resolved in commitment to the possibility's 'reality'.

And once that time is over, we are faced with the logic of its consequences. So we must turn now to our final two parables, which address the 'what happens next' of that logic.

13 The Parables of 'The Last Judgement' and 'The Great Banquet' (introduced by 'The Seats of Honour')

'The Last Judgement' (Matt. 25:31–46)

This, one of the best known and possibly most influential of the parables, appears only in Matthew, but in places bears strong family resemblances to passages from Chapter 7 of the prophet Daniel on the one hand, and the Books of Jude (v. 14) and Revelation (20:11) on the other. Before glancing at some of this we need to notice that the story is part of a sequence of parables introduced by Matthew through Jesus' discussion with his disciples (after he has foretold the fall of the Temple) about the signs of his own 'coming' and of 'the end of the age'. He foretells upheavals and agitations which are to come, 'but the end is not yet', not, in fact, till 'this good news of the kingdom' is 'proclaimed throughout the world'. Then, and only then, 'the end will come'. There follow details of the drama of that 'end', supported by a series of parables, part of whose point is in an unlooked-for, unexpected 'coming' which precipitates crisis ('The Temporary Manager', 'The Ten Bridesmaids', 'The Talents'). As a conclusion to this sequence he tells the parable of 'The Last Judgement' and as a coda to that, Matthew places (what now appears as the first two verses of the next chapter) Jesus' reminder to his disciples – which is presumably recorded with hindsight, but not taken seriously at the time – that they know 'after two days the Passover is coming, and the Son of Man will be handed over to be crucified'.

So the story is the climax to teaching about the coming End-Time, and itself points forward to what is actually a decisive act of 'Judgement': the Crucifixion. For just as the *presence* of Jesus in the world is *itself* a judgement on the world (John 9:39; 12:31–33), so the Crucifixion is the final stage of this particular act of judgement. Its nature is so totally different from the apocalyptic language of the End-Time we find recorded *passim* in the Bible, that we must guard against missing its reality as one of the ways in which God enacts his Judgement. We need to bear it in mind, therefore, as we read this parable of 'The Last Judgement'.

The story

The parable itself is in three parts. Its first stage is that same 'coming' of the 'Son of Man' the discussion of which between Jesus and the disciples prefaces this sequence of teaching. Its detail breaks through the metonymy of realism: we are in the context here of a different, but just as familiar, metonymy, that of apocalypse and its aftermath. Inevitably this leads to cross-over language, since though it is part of an integrated whole, that of the coherent familiar 'story' of the last point of End-Time before deliverance into eternity, yet it also carries a meta-phoric mode – as we shall see – that speaks of *contemporary* life when lived 'in the kingdom'.

The material familiar to Jesus' listeners which informs all three stages of the parable is found most notably in Daniel 7, with its references to the glory of the 'Ancient One' coming in brilliant white light and fire, served by 'a thousand thousand', as he takes his throne of 'fiery flames' and 'the court sat in judgment'. This Ancient One is (7:13) approached by 'one like a son of man', who comes 'with the clouds of heaven', and to him is given 'dominion' and 'kingship'.

The equivalent of the brilliance and throng of servants, in our parable, is in the word 'glory' and the description of his servants as 'his angels with him'. The first stage of the story ends as he takes his throne, which is at once that of both 'royalty' and 'judgement'.

The second stage is the actual Judgement itself. That is, all the prelude of catastrophe is concluded. This is now the resolution following victory, where like and unlike are distinguished. A homely pastoral image links this apocalyptic world, coherent in its own metonymy, with the metonymy of ordinary life. For this Judge's action is summarised as 'like' something familiar to every Palestinian listener: the evening-time separation of the sheep and goats which have grazed together all day. A separation arising from their different needs – the goats for shelter, the sheep for air. It is *this* reminder of a realistic metonymic world which helps the parable to work, for this world where sheep and goats have to be separated and dealt with each evening is the same world where men and women are compassionate and careful of each other, or not; the world where there are hungry to whom some give food, out of care and kindness; where there are similarly those who are thirsty, or strangers, or in tattered rags, or lying sick, or fastened away in prison. And some care for them, and some are wholly careless of them. It is a coherent, recognisable, consistent world, a metonymic world we are instantly familiar with.

And so would be Jesus' listeners. The 'good deeds' laid out are in no way revolutionary, but part of regular Jewish teaching on the responsibilities that attached to the nation's religious calling. Regularly observable, too, in the texture of life in village and town. Equally familiar is the *other* metonymic world, that of the apocalyptic story, with the King on his throne, giving Judgement that is ultimate on 'all the nations gathered before him'.

But the metaphoric mode takes us further into this parable. For since Jesus regularly uses the title of 'Son of Man' of himself, it follows that he is claiming a role in the final Judgement that is normally in Jewish teaching ascribed to God, the Ancient One (as is, regularly the 'throne' of 'royalty' and 'judgement'). That God, nevertheless, retains Judgement and Sovereignty is implied in this Son's reference to him when addressing the 'righteous': 'Come, you that are blessed by my Father . . .'. But it is Jesus who *enacts* this ultimate judgement; just as he had 'enacted judgement' by his very presence on earth, and by his suffering the Crucifixion.

What is it that makes these called out to his right hand 'blessed'? They have carried out works of compassionate kindness; yes, but there is more than this. For a work of kindness to 'one of the least of these who are members of my family' (or 'these my brothers') is a work of kindness 'to Christ himself'.

This is where the story departs from fairly similar Jewish stories of 'good' living. For Jesus is thereby claiming at one and the same time to be 'one with' *both* the Son of Man on God's royal throne of judgement *and* the hungry, thirsty, poor, naked, imprisoned stranger who is the object of pity and compassionate care.

Some have argued that the use of the term 'these my brothers' or 'these who are members of my family' is in fact a reference to his followers, and that the early Church would hear the story this way, i.e., that it is those who care for the needs of the suffering young Christian community and its members who find themselves 'blessed' by the Father of the Lord Jesus Christ whose cause they serve.

While it seems quite possible the early Church may have interpreted the story in such a way, it seems an unnecessarily narrow reading of the parable. For here metaphor and metonymy cross, in that Jesus did literally become not only a 'stranger' in his wanderings through his teaching ministry, but hungry, thirsty and poor. And at the last he was naked and imprisoned. So that *literally* he has become one of those for whom the compassionate care of his fellow human beings is wholly appropriate.

Yet at *the very same time* he resolutely refuses to deny his claim to the status of the Son of God who shall, indeed, share in the judging of humanity. And an earnest of this is to be found in the Crucifixion. Here is judgement by absoluteness of suffering; power surrendered to the point of extinction; status surrendered to the point of total humiliation. This is the *obverse* of that *reverse* which is the 'Son of Man' coming in glory with his angels and taking his royal throne of judgement. In other words, the world is as judged by divine Mercy as it is by divine Justice. It is *Jesus* who enacts that ultimate point at which they meet.

The third stage

The heart of the parable is the act of 'judging' itself, and the equally surprised response of the 'righteous' and the 'wicked'. The 'judging' has *begun* by separating 'like' from 'unlike'. We are left in no doubt that Jesus saw a sifting of humanity as an essential element in that final 'setting right' of things which is the nature of the final consummation of human history. That which distinguishes those in the places of honour as sentence begins to be passed – those on the right hand – is that they have been 'doing the will of the Father' in responding to his Son in his kinship with the suffering and the poor. But, with hindsight, since the Crucifixion is a preliminary 'act of judgement', we may include amongst the 'blessed' those who have responded, with anguished compassion, to the suffering, thirsty prisoner dying on the Cross, both directly and as they have known him in the disadvantaged persons among whom they live.

They are 'to inherit the kingdom prepared for [them] from the foundation of the world'. That is, they have by their manner of life and the heart's attitude from which it springs, claimed their continuum with that relationship with the Creator God which has inhered since creation. They are rooted in the long history of the family of God, back to the very 'foundation of the world'.

Their opposites are those for whom the notion of compassion has no place, who have not recognised Christ in his sufferings, or his presence in the needy around them. They therefore have cast off that family relationship as meaningless, which Jesus explicitly described, gesturing to the poor, exigent, yearning crowd, hanging on his words as they sat round him: 'Here are my mother and my brothers! Whoever does the will of God is my brother and sister and mother' (Mark 3:34, 35; cf. Matt. 12:49, 50; Luke 8:19–21). For such, glimpsing at the last the possibility from which they have for ever excluded themselves, 'fire' is as vivid an image as could be found for that self-consuming anger which did not want what it could have had, until it could no longer have it; which misjudged totally where 'obedience' to 'good' lay, so that consequently the roots withered away and died that were the vital connections to the continuum of creative life with God.

Hence they have no place in the 'prepared kingdom'. We shall meet them again in our last parable, 'The Great Banquet'. But with them we shall meet also those entering with joy into their own inheritance. With them, we are given one further glimpse into the nature of the Last Things; a future not just for those first listeners to Jesus, not even the early Church assembling and pondering on his teachings and stories; but for us, two millennia further on. For us, preparing to celebrate a second millennium from that moment at which divine Judgement was made flesh, and dwelt among us.

'The Great Banquet' (and 'The Seats of Honour') (Matt. 22:1–10; Luke 14:16–24 with 14:7–11)

This story of the End-Time appears in both Matthew and Luke, though in different settings, with differing details, and with different emphases. In Matthew it is introduced by the familiar phrase 'the kingdom of heaven is like . . .' and in Luke by the (one suspects over-pious) comment to Jesus by a fellow dinner guest, 'Blessed is anyone who will eat bread in the kingdom of God!' The story is Jesus' direct and unprefaced reply to this.

In fact in Luke the story is part of a sequence of comment and questions offered in the context of a 'luncheon or dinner' (14:12) where Jesus is a guest. The sequence begins with the healing of a man suffering from dropsy who is 'in front of him' as he goes to eat a meal on the Sabbath at the house of a leader of the Pharisees. The action is controversial: Jesus challenges the religious leaders among his fellow guests who 'were watching him closely', about the lawfulness of healing, of rescue, on the Sabbath day. They 'were silent', for 'they could not reply to this'.

So what follows comes in an atmosphere of contention arising from directly opposed understandings of what the Law means in terms of obedience to God's will, and the life-style consequent upon that understanding. We are to envisage the group, after this incident on the way to the house, arriving there. At once, as Jesus notices, the guests begin to 'choose places of honour'. Out of this he draws what Luke designates 'a parable', concerning 'seats of honour'. The metonymic mode of this and of what follows (including the parable of 'The Great Banquet' itself) is shaped within the local culture of hospitality at meals, instantly recognisable to Jesus' listeners.

The metonymy of hospitality

In the parable of 'The Seats of Honour' Jesus is noting what regularly happens when guests are filing into the banqueting chamber. There is a silent but nevertheless real struggle for 'status', carried out by identifying and occupying the 'top table' – the 'seats of honour', wherever they may be. Behind this lies an assumption that such 'honour' is there for the taking, a matter of self-designation, i.e., if one is confident enough, and ruthless enough, the implied 'honour' can be

gained and held on to. But – as must have happened from time
to time, and may even have been an actual incident known to
Jesus' listeners – there will on occasion be present someone
genuinely 'distinguished'. How shaming if because of one's
greed for 'status' public attention is drawn to one's comparative
lack of distinction, as the host publicly requests one to make
way for the more important guest and move to a lowlier place.

Behind this local metonymy lies something which does not
change in human society, a sort of constant 'metonymy'. The
social event as a kind of strategy, in which the purpose is not
so much to give pleasure to others, either as guest or host, but
to establish a particular social position. Hence the adjuration
which follows, which would appear to have arisen from a
further invitation to Jesus by a fellow guest. The ritual round
of giving and receiving invitations, the local colour of which
may vary from place to place and century to century, but the
essence of which remains unchanged to our own day and place,
is for many, Jesus points out, essentially a part of this establishing and maintaining of 'position'. So those invited are one's
'friends or brothers or relatives or rich neighbours' (14:12); and
the assumption is that such an invitation will trigger a return
invitation, and so the process will go on, and the host will 'be
repaid'. (One is reminded of Christ's comment on those who
'practise their piety before others in order to be seen by them'
i.e., for social reasons: 'They have received', says Jesus, 'their
reward' (Matt. 6:2, 5, 16).)

Something of this metonymy of hospitality informs the
parable of 'The Great Banquet', as we shall see. But, as with
this preliminary material in Luke, it is also a 'way into' the
metaphoric mode in which Jesus is pointing to what is truly
involved in the Law. For what is involved in the Law is as
different from this social formalising of hospitality, as his
healing, rescuing, of a fellow human being on the Sabbath is,
from the formal, rigorously externalised, 'keeping of the
Sabbath holy' demanded by his opponents.

The metaphoric mode of hospitality

Returning to the parable about the struggle for 'seats of
honour', one bridge into the metaphoric mode is that Jesus
makes the occasion the parable describes a 'wedding banquet'.
This, besides being a regular part of the familiar metonymy of

everyday Palestinian life, is also part of the metonymy of Jewish religious language: it is a regular image of God's festive celebration for his loved ones at the End-Time. So it is crossover language into the metaphor of life lived in eternity. We therefore may read this as a challenge to have the appropriate attitude of heart at the prospect of the great feast of heaven. The Jewish nation as a whole in its special relationship to God is 'invited'; so, of course, are its religious leaders. *Especially* so, they would imagine. So the parable becomes a warning. Do not assume that the 'seats of honour' in heaven are yours for the taking, by strategy, or assumption of prior right. For, unknown to you, there may well be guests of far greater distinction in terms of the Kingdom of heaven, than yourself. Then, inevitably, you would endure the public humiliation of being sent lower. Therefore wisdom would suggest a real humility about one's deserts which would lead one naturally to take a lowly seat in the banqueting hall. If God the host adjudges you worthy of greater position, he will ensure it. And how much more honouring to be placed by *him* in the higher position, rather than by your own estimation!

But there is a little more, and the sequential reference to reasons for inviting guests helps us to it. For if the ritual formal pattern, with its brittle social rewards, of giving and receiving guests of one's own or higher status, is to be transformed, then that can only be done by hospitality from the heart. That is, the offering of hospitality not because people socially 'desire' it, or because it will enhance one's own social position, but to give pure pleasure to those who can in no way return hospitality. This carries a quite different 'reward', that of the 'righteous' in the Kingdom of heaven which is eternal.

Now such a banquet, where the host freely wines and dines for their delight those who could not possibly repay, is of course a model, an image, of God's own great Banquet of the End-Time for those he gathers to it. Hence those who behave likewise in their hospitable living out of the Law have entered into the spirit which informs the End-Time, have shown a 'family-likeness' to the God who is their Father.

And it is such an attitude which needs to inform them as *guests*, as well as *hosts*. As 'hosts' their joy should come, as God's does, from giving pleasure and sustenance to those who cannot return it; as 'guests' their chief joy should be to be *present*, with

no assumptions about status. For such an attitude of heart is
an essential attribute of those who belong to the family of God,
destined to join him in the great feast of heaven.

'The Great Banquet': differences between Luke and Matthew
The context Matthew gives to the parable of 'The Great Banquet'
is in many ways different from Luke's but the tension between
Jesus and the religious leaders is a constant. Matthew places
the story after the Pharisees, having listened to the parable of
'The Usurping Tenants', 'realised that he was speaking about
them'.

There are features of the parable itself, however, which differ
quite sharply between the two gospel versions. In Matthew it
is a 'king' who is giving a 'wedding banquet' for his son: the
climax of the parable is 'so the wedding hall was filled with
guests'. To this has been added another parable, that of 'The
Guest Without a Wedding Garment', which we read in an
earlier chapter.

Luke's host is not a 'king', but 'someone who gave a great
dinner, and invited many'. So the metonymy is different, Luke's
being much more that of familiar Palestinian life, Matthew's
that of traditional storytelling. As the parable proceeds, there
are further differences. Luke's host sends out one servant to
indicate the feast is ready, Matthew's king sends out several,
and, when they are rejected, sends out more. Then Matthew
introduces a complication into the plot quite absent from Luke:
the second group of servants are 'maltreated and killed'. In
rage the king sends his troops 'who destroyed those murderers
and burned the city'. Meantime, the feast is still waiting and
ready!

There follows the sending out of 'servants' by the king in
Matthew's account, 'a' servant by the host of Luke's account,
to bring into the feast folk not previously invited. Here Luke's
version sends out twice, and Matthew's only once. In both cases
the intention is that the 'house be filled': and not with those
previously invited, for 'they were not worthy' (Matthew); 'none
of them . . . will taste my dinner' (Luke).

The metonymy of 'The Great Banquet'
Following up the detail of these two versions, it is worth
noticing the degree of consistency with recognisable, familiar

life in both, even in Matthew. There was indeed a courteous custom of the country that when the feast was ready a servant was sent to usher those previously invited to the meal. Moreover, the reasons for not attending are not remote and unlikely, but daily preoccupations. In Matthew they are briefly summarised: they 'made light of [the summons] and went away, one to his farm, another to his business' (22:5); a response much more fully fleshed out in Luke's version, where one has bought a piece of land, and 'must go out and see it', and another must do the same with his recently bought 'five yoke of oxen'. The third excuse is almost certainly pure humour: 'I have just been married, and therefore I cannot come.' With the exception of this last it is arguable that these were not absolute refusals but apologies for a very delayed arrival. The banquet could be relied upon to continue late, and meantime the daylight hours must be used for more vital matters – estate and business affairs. Perhaps the key is in the phrase, 'They made light of it'. The summons to the feast, that is, is not seen as of primary importance in their lives.

More detail, building up the metonymic picture, is to be found in the sending out of the servants to bring in those not invited. Matthew's servants are to go into the 'main streets' – that is, the wider areas or squares into which the narrow lanes debouch – where people congregate and can most easily be gathered. Luke's servant is sent out twice to gather people in. First into 'the streets and lanes of the town' where the social outcasts live – 'the poor, crippled, blind and lame'; and then into the 'roads and lanes', that is, the network of paths coming through the countryside, where the same categories of derelict humanity would either be sheltering under the hedges and walls, or travelling towards the towns to beg. They would represent possibly an even lower level of social outcast, since they would almost certainly be homeless.

The metaphoric mode

Thus far the material, in both versions, resonates either with the metonymy of familiar life, or with that of traditional storytelling (the 'complication' in Matthew's account of the killing of the servants, the sending of the troops and the razing of the city, is the familiar material either of folk tale or of legendary punitive expeditions the land had certainly suffered in past times). But what of the metaphoric mode?

To get at the heart of this we need to establish the basic story. A great banquet has been prepared, to which many have been invited in advance. But when the critical moment arrives, the guests are unprepared for it, and it is not as important to them as their immediate preoccupations. So they either temporise, or actually decline the opportunity. Their host is clear that no further chance should be given them. But the feast is prepared, and he is going to hold his celebration: for it is in *his* time, not his guests'. So he gathers in crowds who would not normally have dreamt of inclusion in such a gathering, 'both good and bad' (Matt. 22:10). The ultimate point is that the hall is full, the banquet is held and *the celebration goes forward*.

Thus the core parable. If we now look at it in the context, in both accounts, of open tension with the religious leaders about what obedience to God according to the Law really meant; and to that add the various themes about hospitality which Luke introduces as a preface, we find ourselves moving into the parable's metaphoric mode. For it concerns those who 'take for granted', as invited to God's great feast in the End-Time, their status as privileged guests. They so take that status for granted that they have become complacent about it, and are not ready – or prepared to make themselves ready – when the summons comes. The summons is away from their social and business preoccupations to that critical encounter with God which should issue in feasting and joy. But they have lost their sense of what is the true priority: readiness to respond to the summons. So they prevaricate. And this unreadiness, and refusal to recognise their unreadiness, 'making light of it', means they will miss for ever that opportunity they had so long taken for granted. For they have not recognised the significance of the moment when it has come.

For Jesus' first listeners the reference to the End-Time would be clear enough, and they would recognise something of the warning to those who would assume that the 'seats of honour' would be theirs, whenever they chose, in the kingdom of eternity. Such was the expectation of many concerning their own presumptuous nation, and its even more presumptuous leaders. But they would not necessarily recognise in 'the servant sent to summon them' the one actually telling the story, the Jesus who sat beside them at dinner. The early Church would make this connection, however, and would no doubt see in the two sets of servants sent out in Matthew's account, first the prophets, and then John the Baptist and Jesus. While in Luke's account they would see the two groups gathered in, the first from the towns and the second from 'beyond', as being first the outcasts of Jewish religious society – tax-gatherers and prostitutes – and, second, the non-Jews, the Gentiles.

The story for today

But the story takes us further than this semi-allegorical, rather mechanistic 'reading'. For we must not lose sight of the preface given by Luke. The categories of derelict humanity invited to fill the hall in Luke – 'the poor, the crippled, the lame and the blind' – are precisely the categories Jesus presses his listeners to make their guests at their own celebrations for no reward but that of 'goodness' ('righteousness'). But we have already noted, in our reading of the parable of 'The Last Judgement', that Jesus makes *himself* at one with such outcasts. We are therefore being pressed to recognise in such entertainment a hospitality to the Lord himself. And this is deliberately ironic, for there are glimpses throughout the gospels of Jesus being entertained not out of warmth of hospitality and genuine longing to serve him and give him pleasure (such as we see in the story of Zacchaeus, Luke 9:5) but for his celebratory (or notoriety) value (as with Simon the Pharisee, Luke 7:36–48). Therefore the challenge to 'feast', out of pure joy, the needy and the suffering, is a challenge to involvement in the very act of redemption: looking to discover in the action no 'status' of any kind, but a *sharing of one's table with the Lord and those he makes his family*. The eucharistic implications are moving and powerful.

And there is more. For the Great Banquet of God is a feast and celebration of homecoming *after* that sifting out, that distinguishing of 'like' from 'unlike', which is the Last Judgement. What this parable suggests is that in a real sense those invited *enact this sifting out for themselves*. Some have invitations, but are 'unprepared', in readiness of spirit, to respond positively to the critical and decisive encounter with God. Some do not even recognise it as the summons to encounter. Some are spiritually indolent; some are complacent, having lost all sense of urgency.

Whatever the causes, their perception of 'the moment' is dull, and they let it pass by.

Those others who take their place have never thought of themselves as 'fit' guests, and so have to be gathered in, even 'compelled', by the sheer authority and force of the invitation, to come in. It is a thought which addresses all missionary enterprise very powerfully. For God continues to send his servant(s) today, through the Church, into the main concourse, into the streets of the city and the roads and lanes of country far and near. How 'compellingly' (Luke 14:23) is the invitation delivered?

Finally, the climax of both versions of the parable is that the 'house' of heaven will be full, the 'wedding hall filled with guests'. That is, after the sorting-out, the painful (self-?) selection which the absoluteness of the moment demands, the feast is certain. The celebration will take place, eternity is secure as an experience of joy. And that is why these parables of the Last Things must surely, in the end, be read as stories of hope, parables of promise, assurances of the warmth of welcome of God the Father to all those who, with yearning, respond to his invitation. Yes, there is warning: but that warning is meant to give pause so that hearts and lives can be changed, and the choice made to go to the Banquet. Only complacency, self-righteousness, or rejection of the messenger can close down our options. The whole sweep of the parables is an exposition of what the life and the 'signs' and the death and the rising of Jesus were enacting amongst humanity. For so many of us thought the feast was not for us, and it was, and the coming of Jesus gave us the entrance. Or we knew the feast was for us, but forgot the wonder that attended that; and the coming of Jesus opened our hearts again to that wonder. Only those not open to either wonder or humility exclude themselves from the Banquet: for it is established by Judgement, but spread before us in Mercy. That is how the parables 'read'.

Epilogue

14 Reflections on the Parables: 'So That They Should Set Their Hope in God'

How HAS OUR READING of the parables deepened our knowledge of the Jesus of history, who lived and died in a certain place at a certain time, and who was afterwards seen alive, in specific places on specific occasions, by those who had known him before his death? How has it deepened our knowledge of the sovereign God through the living Lord Jesus, whose risen life we have ourselves experienced?

The time and place

The parables give us very clearly an authenticity of time and place. They are couched in pictures and images and dialogue and incidents which have the local colour. To *this* culture, at *this* time, the man Jesus belonged. An agrarian culture of crops and vineyards and sheep and goat-keeping, of lakeside villages where the fishermen lived and from which they went out to catch their fish – or toil all night and catch nothing. A land of small villages and larger towns and slightly larger cities, where people were very rich sometimes and lived sumptuously and wined and dined each other at banquets. Or very poor sometimes, and begged in the streets. Towns and villages where ordinary domestic life went on, marked by the many minor crises which make up life: running out of oil for the lamps, losing some coins in a dark corner of the house, being knocked up late at night by unlooked-for visitors, running short of bread . . . Towns and villages where weddings and funerals more dramatically marked the passage of time, their processions imitated by the children playing in the marketplace. That same marketplace where at harvest time casual labour gathered, hoping to be hired as the hours crept by under the hot Palestinian sun – third hour, sixth hour, ninth hour . . .

A land where courts were held and judges gave rulings and sometimes, even if you were a vulnerable widow, the judgement was in your favour; and sometimes it was penally against you and you went to gaol. A land of some large estates where middle management was faithful and hardworking and incorruptible, or indolent, bullying and corrupt: estates where some employers treated their slaves and their hired hands with noteworthy care and generosity, and where there was for the casual labourer a recognised fixed wage. A place where men built houses against the harsher seasons, sometimes well-, sometimes ill-placed. Those same seasons whose coming the weather-wise could foretell by the signs of their coming – the direction of the wind, the buds on the trees. Seasons marked by planting and tending and manuring and weeding and reaping and harvesting. A texture of life constricted by the political realities of being a subject nation, invested militarily and politically by its conquerors. So a land under heavy taxation, with often crooked officials to collect it. Yet in spite of this a national life confident of, even arrogant in, its own identity, shaped as that identity was by a special religious consciousness. So a land whose religious leaders wielded an unassailable authority over the lives of its people. A nation, therefore, where the local synagogue and the great Temple at Jerusalem were significant focal points of personal and national hope and devout practice. Of prayer, and teaching about God . . .

The God Christ declared

All this detail of colour and texture we gain about Jesus and his life, from the parables. But his presence amid such a culture was to declare something about that God who was at the centre of the nation's religious identity. And beyond that (to the religious leaders' displeasure) his presence insistently told out something of God's relationship, not just with this nation, but with humanity beyond it. So the parables aid us in understanding what Jesus' 'presence' in the world was saying about what God is really 'like' in relation to his whole creation.

Moreover, Jesus' presence was *itself* God in action in the world. By his being there, God was 'doing' something. God in action, in Jesus, in the way he lived his life: in his words, and his relationships, and in his 'signs' of power. God in action, in Jesus, in the way he died his death: in what he said, in his relationships as death approached, and in his offering up of his power. And in that breaking through death with renewed and undefeated life, vital with the very power he had willingly laid down, that surging divine vitality which showed so dynamically in his Resurrection words and relationships and actions. In all these, God was 'doing' something. The parables offer us interpretation of what God was doing.

Justice and Mercy

One strong thread runs through what the parables suggest, about 'what God was like' in Jesus and 'what God was doing' through Jesus. That thread is the issue of divine Justice and divine Mercy in relation to humanity, of how they meet in the God Jesus shows us, and are resolved. It is a question as urgent for our generation, as we ponder issues of absolute values or none, as it has ever been for humanity. The nation into which Jesus was born looked to God for ultimate Justice, vindication, at the End-Time, at the consummation of history. In the meantime it attempted to enact justice in the pattern of its national life, a human justice based on what was believed to be divine Law. In his teaching Jesus honours this attempt where it comes from the heart and seeks to serve God rather than subjugate humankind. No 'jot or tittle' of such true justice would be removed.

But he powerfully challenges the narrowing of God's Law to minutiae, to external rigorist observances; or its use to exclude people rather than include them. The parables continually draw our attention to the function of divine Mercy as operative within God's Law *in as absolute a sense* as divine Justice. This is what we see at the Cross: Mercy in action meeting with Justice and resolving it.

Moreover, the parables insist, this should be a matter of profound thanksgiving to those who have sought to be 'absolute' in Justice. For it is the rigorists who are shown in the parables as in need of mercy quite as profoundly as those they had themselves deemed 'outsiders'.

Hence 'complacency' and self-righteousness' are, as the parables interpret, the actual agents of God's critical Judgement, for they foreclose his grace, both for others and for oneself. For oneself, because they shut one off from the sheer surprise and wondering delight which is the heart's best response to the plenitude and inexhaustibility of God's Mercy. Complacency and self-righteousness take us even today – as they took so many of the religious leaders of Jesus' day – out of the main-stream of that *amazement* which is the human experience of divine grace, by a habit of mind of improper confidence. Such 'wrong' – as opposed to 'right' – confidence is rooted not in the nature of the God we have learned to trust, and as we see him in action on Calvary, but in overweening presumptions about our own 'worthiness' and 'adequacy'. And when the heart is no longer in the mainstream of that 'amazing grace' which the parables describe and Jesus' life and death enact, then all that flows from that grace, both into the way we live and the relationships we make and the view we take of other people – all that slowly dries up also.

This is the passionate warning Jesus gives in the parables, the same warning his life and 'signs' and death were about. And it is a warning addressed no less to us today than to those to whom he spoke in the flesh. 'Look at those you deem "outsiders",' he says to all of us who think of ourselves as spiritually 'respectable'. 'See them as a model for how you yourselves actually *are*, before God.' ('For all our righteous-nesses are as filthy rags' (Isa. 64:6, AV).) 'And see too that the Kingdom of heaven is for them, and they stream in through its doors to the Banquet. As you may too; but only if you recognise that before God you are not only *kin* to them, but *belong* to them.'

So this is the hope, the *right* confidence, he is setting before us as his parables interpret the God he was showing in action. The hope of a recovery of our true selves before God, a relation-ship of wondering and amazed delight that we, even we, may be caught up through his Mercy – and *only* through his Mercy – into the courts of heaven and belong in the family of God at the celebratory supper. And with us, all suffering humanity whenever it longs for goodness, knows it fails in it, and looks for rescue to the Father who runs to meet the wistful prodigal. All humanity, whenever it looks with the kindness it has learnt from the kindness of God, on the derelict and despairing, those caught in the trap of poverty, misery, abuse and neglect. For in the kindness of God we discover they are ourselves under the skin, and – as they yearn after him – 'brother, sister, mother' of Christ himself.

'So that they should set their hope in God'
Earlier in this book (in Chapter 10) we noticed a reference by Matthew (14:34, 35) to Jesus' use of parables as a teaching method, 'to fulfil', as that gospel put it, 'what had been spoken through the prophet Isaiah'. What is actually quoted there is (rather endearingly) not from Isaiah, but from Psalm 78, verse 2. As we conclude this reading of the parables of Jesus it is worth dwelling on this part of the Psalm, for it gives us a crucial perspective. Psalm 78:2–7a reads:

> I will open my mouth in a parable;
>   I will utter dark sayings from of old,
> things that we have heard and known,
>   that our ancestors have told us.
> We will not hide them from their children;
>   we will tell to the coming generation
> the glorious deeds of the Lord, and his might,
>   and the wonders that he has done.
>
> He established a decree in Jacob,
>   and appointed a law in Israel,
> Which he commanded our ancestors
>   to teach to their children;
> that the next generation might know them,
>   the children yet unborn,
> and rise up and tell them to their children,
>   so that they should set their hope in God.

'So that they should set their hope in God.' That, in the end, is what the parables were meant to do. Direct the eyes of those who heard Jesus, and all the generations who have listened to these stories since, to the hope that is in God. They are a living and lasting commentary by Christ himself on his own ministry, on his message, on the purpose of his presence, on the necessity and power of his suffering and on the glory of his rising. They tell us of the true and lively hope which is ours because God is the God of the parables: trustworthy, unsleeping, tender, setting no limits to his Mercy (and not allowing humanity to prescribe such limits either). And yet a God who will uphold the right, in which the consummation of human history will be a 'setting right' of that which disfigures or mars humanity's relationship with him. That consummation, that 'Last Judgement', has been prefigured in the 'setting right' of the Cross, where divine Justice was absorbed in divine Mercy, that all who would might gather round the Table, the Feast, the Banquet. These are 'the glorious deeds of the Lord', and 'wonders he has done', beyond any conceiving of the Psalmist.

Therefore, as we return to the parables, it is to see them as documents of hope for humankind. And as such, rooted as they now are for us in the living hope that is our experience of Christ, they are our gift to pass on, to 'children yet unborn', 'the coming generation'. For they speak of a God of such radical love that each generation needs to discover afresh, in its own reading of the parables, with wonder, what God is truly 'like'. And how he has entered and become part of the small, closed metonymic world which is the personal life of each one of us, down through the ages, till that foretold End – whatever and whenever it is – shall come.

Index